Henry IV

(John S. C. Abbott)

KARTINDO PUBLISHING HOUSE (Kartindo.Com)

PREFACE

History is our Heaven-appointed instructor. It is the guide for the future. The calamities of yesterday are the protectors of to-day.

The sea of time we navigate is full of perils. But it is not an unknown sea. It has been traversed for ages, and there is not a sunken rock or a treacherous sand-bar which is not marked by the wreck of those who have preceded us.

There is no portion of history fraught with more valuable instruction than the period of those terrible religious wars which desolated the sixteenth century. There is no romance so wild as the veritable history of those times. The majestic outgoings of the Almighty, as developed in the onward progress of our race, infinitely transcend, in all the elements of profoundness, mystery, and grandeur, all that man's fancy can create.

The cartoons of Raphael are beautiful, but what are they when compared with the heaving ocean, the clouds of sunset, and the pinnacles of the Alps? The dome of St. Peter's is man's noblest architecture, but what is it when compared with the magnificent rotunda of the skies?

JOHN S. C. ABBOTT.

Brunswick, Maine, 1856.

KARTINDO PUBLISHING HOUSE (Kartindo.Com)

CONTENTS

I. CHILDHOOD AND YOUTH

II. CIVIL WAR

III. THE MARRIAGE

IV. PREPARATIONS FOR MASSACRE

V. MASSACRE OF ST. BARTHOLOMEW

VI. THE HOUSES OF VALOIS, OF GUISE, AND OF BOURBON

VII. REIGN OF HENRY III

VIII. THE LEAGUE

IX. THE ASSASSINATION OF THE DUKE OF GUISE AND OF HENRY III

X. WAR AND WOE

XI. THE CONVERSION OF THE KING

XII. THE REIGN OF HENRY IV. AND HIS DEATH

KARTINDO PUBLISHING HOUSE (Kartindo.Com)

CHAPTER I

CHILDHOOD AND YOUTH

1475-1564

Navarre.--Catharine de Foix.--Ferdinand and Isabella.--Dismemberment of Navarre.--Plans for revenge.--Death of Catharine.--Marriage of Henry and Margaret.--Lingering hopes of Henry.--Jeanne returns to Navarre.--Birth of Henry IV.--The royal nurse.--Name chosen for the young prince.--The castle of Courasse.--Education of Henry.--Death of the King of Navarre.--Jeanne d'Albret ascends the throne.--Residence in Bearn.--Marriage of Mary, Queen of Scots.--Betrothal of Henry.--Henry's tutor.--Remark of Dr. Johnson.--Henry's motto.--La Gaucherie's method of instruction.--Death of Henry II.--Catharine de Medicis regent.--Influence of Plutarch.--Religious agitation.--The Huguenots.--The present controversy.--The Sorbonne.--Purging the empire.-- The burning chamber.--Persecution of the Protestants.--Calvin and his writings.--Calvin's physical debility.--Continued labors.--Execution of Servetus.--Inhabitants of France.--Antony of Bourbon.--Jeanne d'Albret.--The separation.--Different life.--Rage of the Pope.--Growth of Protestantism.-- Catharine's blandishments.--Undecided action.--Seizure of the queen.--Civil war.--Death of Antony of Bourbon.--Effects of the war.--Liberty of worship.-- Indignation and animosity.--Religious toleration.--Belief of the Romanists.-- Establishment of freedom of conscience.

About four hundred years ago there was a small kingdom, spreading over the cliffs and ravines of the eastern extremity of the Pyrenees, called Navarre. Its population, of about five hundred thousand, consisted of a very simple, frugal, and industrious people. Those who lived upon the shore washed by the stormy waves of the Bay of Biscay gratified their love of excitement and of adventure by braving the perils of the sea. Those who lived in the solitude of the interior, on the sunny slopes of the mountains, or by the streams which meandered through the verdant valleys, fed their flocks, and harvested their grain, and pressed rich wine from the grapes of their vineyards, in the enjoyment of the most pleasant duties of rural life. Proud of their independence, they were ever ready to grasp arms to repel foreign aggression. The throne of this kingdom was, at the time of which we speak, occupied by Catharine de Foix. She was a widow, and all her hopes and affections were centred in her son Henry, an ardent and impetuous boy six or seven years of age, who was to receive the crown when it should fall from her brow, and transmit to posterity their ancestral honors.

Ferdinand of Aragon had just married Isabella of Castile, and had thus united those two populous and wealthy kingdoms; and now, in the arrogance of power, seized with the pride of annexation, he began to look with a wistful eye upon the picturesque kingdom of Navarre. Its comparative feebleness, under the reign of a bereaved woman weary of the world, invited to the enterprise. Should he grasp at the whole territory of the little realm, France might interpose her powerful remonstrance. Should he take but the half which was spread out upon the southern declivity of the Pyrenees, it would be virtually saying to the French monarch, "The rest I courteously leave for you." The armies of Spain were soon sweeping resistlessly through these sunny valleys, and one half of her empire was ruthlessly torn from the Queen of Navarre, and transferred to the dominion of imperious Castile and Aragon.

Catharine retired with her child to the colder and more uncongenial regions of the northern declivity of the mountains. Her bosom glowed with mortification and rage in view of her hopeless defeat. As she sat down gloomily in the small portion which remained to her of her dismembered empire, she endeavored to foster in the heart of her son the spirit of revenge, and to inspire him with the resolution to regain those lost leagues of territory which had been wrested from the inheritance of his fathers. Henry imbibed his mother's spirit, and chafed and fretted under wrongs for which he could obtain no redress. Ferdinand and Isabella could not be annoyed even by any force which feeble Navarre could raise. Queen Catharine, however, brooded deeply over her wrongs, and laid plans for retributions of revenge, the execution of which she knew must be deferred till long after her body should have mouldered to dust in the grave. She courted the most intimate alliance with Francis I., King of France. She contemplated the merging of her own little kingdom into that powerful monarchy, that the infant Navarre, having grown into the giant France, might crush the Spanish tyrants into humiliation. Nerved by this determined spirit of revenge, and inspired by a mother's ambition, she intrigued to wed her son to the heiress of the French throne, that even in the world of spirits she might be cheered by seeing Henry heading the armies of France, the terrible avenger of her wrongs. These hopes invigorated her until the fitful dream of her joyless life was terminated, and her restless spirit sank into the repose of the grave. She lived, however, to see her plans apparently in progress toward their most successful fulfillment.

KARTINDO PUBLISHING HOUSE (Kartindo.Com)

Henry, her son, was married to Margaret, the favorite sister of the King of France. Their nuptials were blessed with but one child, Jeanne d'Albret. This child, in whose destiny such ambitious hopes were centred, bloomed into most marvelous beauty, and became also as conspicuous for her mental endowments as for her personal charms. She had hardly emerged from the period of childhood when she was married to Antony of Bourbon, a near relative of the royal family of France. Immediately after her marriage she left Navarre with her husband, to take up her residence in the French metropolis.

One hope still lived, with undying vigor, in the bosom of Henry. It was the hope, the intense passion, with which his departed mother had inspired him, that a grandson would arise from this union, who would, with the spirit of Hannibal, avenge the family wrongs upon Spain. Twice Henry took a grandson into his arms with the feeling that the great desire of his life was about to be realized; and twice, with almost a broken heart, he saw these hopes blighted as he committed the little ones to the grave.

Summers and winters had now lingered wearily away, and Henry had become an old man. Disappointment and care had worn down his frame. World-weary and joyless, he still clung to hope. The tidings that Jeanne was again to become a mother rekindled the lustre of his fading eye. The aged king sent importunately for his daughter to return without delay to the paternal castle, that the child might be born in the kingdom of Navarre, whose wrongs it was to be his peculiar destiny to avenge. It was mid-winter. The journey was long and the roads rough. But the dutiful and energetic Jeanne promptly obeyed the wishes of her father, and hastened to his court.

Henry could hardly restrain his impatience as he waited, week after week, for the advent of the long-looked-for avenger. With the characteristic superstition of the times, he constrained his daughter to promise that, at the period of birth, during the most painful moments of her trial, she would sing a mirthful and triumphant song, that her child might possess a sanguine, joyous, and energetic spirit.

Henry entertained not a doubt that the child would prove a boy, commissioned by Providence as the avenger of Navarre. The old king received the child, at the moment of its birth, into his own arms, totally regardless of a mother's rights, and exultingly enveloping it in soft folds, bore it off, as his own property, to his private apartment. He rubbed the lips of the plump little boy with garlic, and then taking a golden goblet of generous wine, the rough and royal nurse forced the beverage he loved so well down the untainted throat of his new-born heir.

"A little good old wine," said the doting grandfather, "will make the boy vigorous, and brave."

We may remark, in passing, that it was *wine*, rich and pure: not that mixture of all abominations, whose only vintage is in cellars, sunless, damp, and fetid, where guilty men fabricate poison for a nation.

[Illustration: THE BIRTH OF HENRY IV.]

This little stranger received the ancestral name of Henry. By his subsequent exploits he filled the world with his renown. He was the first of the Bourbon line who ascended the throne of France, and he swayed the sceptre of energetic rule over that wide-spread realm with a degree of power and grandeur which none of his descendants have ever rivaled. The name of Henry IV. is one of the most illustrious in the annals of France. The story of his struggles for the attainment of the throne of Charlemagne is full of interest. His birth, to which we have just alluded, occurred at Parr, in the kingdom of Navarre, in the year 1553.

His grandfather immediately assumed the direction of every thing relating to the child, apparently without the slightest consciousness that either the father or the mother of Henry had any prior claims. The king possessed, among the wild and romantic fastnesses of the mountains, a strong old castle, as rugged and frowning as the eternal granite upon which its foundations were laid. Gloomy evergreens clung to the hill-sides. A mountain stream, often swollen to an impetuous torrent by the autumnal rains and the spring thaws, swept through the little verdant lawn, which smiled amid the stern sublimities surrounding this venerable and moss-covered fortress. Around the solitary towers the eagles wheeled and screamed in harmony with the gales and storms which often swept through these wild regions. The expanse around was sparsely settled by a few hardy peasants, who, by feeding their herds, and cultivating little patches of soil among the crags, obtained a humble living, and by exercise and the pure mountain air acquired a vigor and an athletic-hardihood of frame which had given them much celebrity.

To the storm-battered castle of Courasse, thus lowering in congenial gloom among these rocks, the old king sent the infant Henry to be nurtured as a peasant-boy, that, by frugal fare and exposure to hardship, he might acquire a peasant's robust frame. He resolved that no French delicacies should enfeeble the constitution of this noble child. Bareheaded and barefooted, the young prince, as yet hardly emerging from infancy, rolled upon the grass, played with the poultry, and the dogs, and the sturdy young mountaineers, and plunged into the brook or paddled in the pools of water with which the mountain showers often filled the court-yard. His hair was bleached and his cheeks bronzed by the sun and the wind. Few would have imagined that the unattractive child, with his unshorn locks and in his studiously neglected garb, was the descendant of a long line of kings, and was destined to eclipse them all by the grandeur of his name.

As years glided along he advanced to energetic boyhood, the constant companion, and, in all his sports and modes of life, the equal of the peasant-boys by whom he was surrounded. He hardly wore a better dress than they; he was nourished with the same coarse fare. With them he climbed the mountains, and leaped the streams, and swung upon the trees. He struggled with his youthful competitors in all their athletic games, running, wrestling, pitching the quoit, and tossing the bar. This active out-door exercise gave a relish to the coarse food of the peasants, consisting of brown bread, beef, cheese, and garlic. His grandfather had decided that this regimen was essential for the education of a prince who was to humble the proud monarchy of Spain, and regain the territory which had been so unjustly wrested from his ancestors.

When Henry was about six years of age, his grandfather, by gradual decay, sank sorrowingly into his grave. Consequently, his mother, Jeanne d'Albret, ascended the throne of Navarre. Her husband, Antony of Bourbon, was a rough, fearless old soldier, with nothing to distinguish him from the multitude who do but live, fight, and die. Jeanne and her husband were in Paris at the time of the death of her father. They immediately hastened to Bearn, the capital of Navarre, to take possession of the dominions which had thus descended to them. The little Henry was then brought from his wild mountain home to reside with his mother in the royal palace. Though Navarre was but a feeble kingdom, the grandeur of its court was said to have been unsurpassed, at that time, by that of any other in Europe. The intellectual education of Henry had been almost entirely neglected; but the hardihood of his body had given such vigor and energy to his mind, that he was now prepared to distance in intellectual pursuits, with perfect ease, those whose infantile brains had been overtasked with study.

Henry remained in Bearn with his parents two years, and in that time ingrafted many courtly graces upon the free and fetterless carriage he had acquired among the mountains. His mind expanded with remarkable rapidity, and he became one of the most beautiful and engaging of children.

About this time Mary, Queen of Scots, was to be married to the Dauphin Francis, son of the King of France. Their nuptials were to be celebrated with great magnificence. The King and Queen of Navarre returned to the court of France to attend the marriage. They took with them their son. His beauty and vivacity excited much admiration in the French metropolis. One day the young prince, then but six or seven years of age, came running into the room where his father and Henry II. of France were conversing, and, by his artlessness and grace, strongly attracted the attention of the French monarch. The king fondly took the playful child in his arms, and said affectionately,

"Will you be my son?"

"No, sire, no! that is my father," replied the ardent boy, pointing to the King of Navarre.

"Well, then, will you be my son-in-law?" demanded Henry.

"Oh yes, most willingly," the prince replied.

Henry II. had a daughter Marguerite, a year or two younger than the Prince of Navarre, and it was immediately resolved between the two parents that the young princes should be considered as betrothed.

Soon after this the King and Queen of Navarre, with their son, returned to the mountainous domain which Jeanne so ardently loved. The queen devoted herself assiduously to the education of the young prince, providing for him the ablest teachers whom that age could afford. A gentleman of very distinguished attainments, named La Gaucherie, undertook the general superintendence of his studies. The young prince was at this time an exceedingly energetic, active, ambitious boy, very inquisitive respecting all matters of information, and passionately fond of study.

Dr. Johnson, with his rough and impetuous severity, has said,

"It is impossible to get Latin into a boy unless you flog it into him."

The experience of La Gaucherie, however, did not confirm this sentiment. Henry always went with alacrity to his Latin and his Greek. His judicious teacher did not disgust his mind with long and laborious rules, but introduced him at once to words and phrases, while gradually he developed the grammatical structure of the language. The vigorous mind of Henry, grasping eagerly at intellectual culture, made rapid progress, and he was soon able to read and write both Latin and Greek with fluency, and ever retained the power of quoting, with great facility and appositeness, from the classical writers of Athens and of Rome. Even in these early days he seized upon the Greek phrase [Greek: "*ê nikan ê apothanein*"], *to conquer or to die*, and adopted it for his motto.

La Gaucherie was warmly attached to the principles of the Protestant faith. He made a companion of his noble pupil, and taught him by conversation in pleasant walks and rides as well as by books. It was his practice to have him commit to memory any fine passage in prose or verse which inculcated generous and lofty ideas. The mind of Henry thus became filled with beautiful images and noble sentiments from the classic writers of France. These gems of literature exerted a powerful influence in moulding his character, and he was fond of quoting them as the guide of his life. Such passages as the following were frequently on the lips of the young prince:

"Over their subjects princes bear the rule, But God, more mighty, governs kings themselves."

Soon after the return of the King and Queen of Navarre to their own kingdom, Henry II. of France died, leaving the crown to his son Charles, a feeble boy both in body and in mind. As Charles was but ten or twelve years of age, his mother, Catharine de Medicis, was appointed regent during his minority. Catharine was a woman of great strength of mind, but of the utmost depravity of heart. There was no crime ambition could instigate her to commit from which, in the slightest degree, she would recoil. Perhaps the history of the world retains not another instance in which a mother could so far forget the yearnings of nature as to endeavor, studiously and perseveringly, to deprave the morals, and by vice to enfeeble the constitution of her son, that she might retain the power which belonged to him. This proud and dissolute woman looked with great solicitude upon the enterprising and energetic spirits of the young Prince of Navarre. There were many providential indications that ere long Henry would be a prominent candidate for the throne of France.

Plutarch's Lives of Ancient Heroes has perhaps been more influential than any other uninspired book in invigorating genius and in enkindling a passion for great achievements. Napoleon was a careful student and a great admirer of Plutarch. His spirit was entranced with the grandeur of the Greek and Roman heroes, and they were ever to him as companions and bosom friends. During the whole of his stormy career, their examples animated him, and his addresses and proclamations were often invigorated by happy quotations from classic story. Henry, with similar exaltation of genius, read and re-read the pages of Plutarch with the most absorbing delight. Catharine, with an eagle eye, watched these indications of a lofty mind. Her solicitude was roused lest the young Prince of Navarre should, with his commanding genius, supplant her degenerate house.

At the close of the sixteenth century, the period of which we write, all Europe was agitated by the great controversy between the Catholics and the Protestants. The writings of Luther, Calvin, and other reformers had aroused the attention of the whole Christian world. In England and Scotland the ancient faith had been overthrown, and the doctrines of the Reformation were, in those kingdoms, established. In France, where the writings of Calvin had been extensively circulated, the Protestants had also become quite numerous, embracing generally the most intelligent portion of the populace. The Protestants were in France called Huguenots, but for what reason is not now known. They were sustained by many noble families, and had for their leaders the Prince of Condé, Admiral Coligni, and the house of Navarre. There were arrayed against them the power of the crown, many of the most powerful nobles, and conspicuously the almost regal house of Guise.

It is perhaps difficult for a Protestant to write upon this subject with perfect impartiality, however earnestly he may desire to do so. The lapse of two hundred years has not terminated the great conflict. The surging strife has swept across the ocean, and even now, with more or less of vehemence, rages in all the states of this new world. Though the weapons of blood are laid aside, the mighty controversy is still undecided.

The advocates of the old faith were determined to maintain their creed, and to force all to its adoption, at whatever price. They deemed heresy the greatest of all crimes, and thought--and doubtless many conscientiously thought--that it should be exterminated even by the pains of torture and death. The French Parliament adopted for its motto, "*One religion, one law, one king.*" They declared that two religions could no more be endured in a kingdom than two governments.

At Paris there was a celebrated theological school called the Sorbonne. It included in its faculty the most distinguished doctors of the Catholic Church. The decisions and the decrees of the Sorbonne were esteemed highly

KARTINDO PUBLISHING HOUSE (Kartindo.Com)

authoritative. The views of the Sorbonne were almost invariably asked in reference to any measures affecting the Church.

In 1525 the court presented the following question to the Sorbonne: "*How can we suppress and extirpate the damnable doctrine of Luther from this very Christian kingdom, and purge it from it entirely?*"

The prompt reply was, "*The heresy has already been endured too long. It must be pursued with the extremest rigor, or it will overthrow the throne.*"

Two years after this, Pope Clement VII. sent a communication to the Parliament of Paris, stating,

"It is necessary, in this great and astounding disorder, which arises from the rage of Satan, and from the fury and impiety of his instruments, that every body exert himself to guard the common safety, seeing that this madness would not only embroil and destroy religion, but also all principality, nobility, laws, orders, and ranks."

The Protestants were pursued by the most unrelenting persecution. The Parliament established a court called the *burning chamber*, because all who were convicted of heresy were burned. The estates of those who, to save their lives, fled from the kingdom, were sold, and their children, who were left behind, were pursued with merciless cruelty.

The Protestants, with boldness which religious faith alone could inspire, braved all these perils. They resolutely declared that the Bible taught their faith, and their faith only, and that no earthly power could compel them to swerve from the truth. Notwithstanding the perils of exile, torture, and death, they persisted in preaching what they considered the pure Gospel of Christ. In 1533 Calvin was driven from Paris. When one said to him, "Mass must be true, since it is celebrated in all Christendom;" he replied, pointing to the Bible,

"There is my mass." Then raising his eyes to heaven, he solemnly said, "O Lord, if in the day of judgment thou chargest me with not having been at mass, I will say to thee with truth, 'Lord, thou hast not commanded it. Behold thy law. In it I have not found any other sacrifice than that which was immolated on the altar of the cross.'"

KARTINDO PUBLISHING HOUSE (Kartindo.Com)

In 1535 Calvin's celebrated "Institutes of the Christian Religion" were published, the great reformer then residing in the city of Basle. This great work became the banner of the Protestants of France. It was read with avidity in the cottage of the peasant, in the work-shop of the artisan, and in the chateau of the noble. In reference to this extraordinary man, of whom it has been said,

"On Calvin some think Heaven's own mantle fell, While others deem him instrument of hell,"

Theodore Beza writes, "I do not believe that his equal can be found. Besides preaching every day from week to week, very often, and as much as he was able, he preached twice every Sunday. He lectured on theology three times a week. He delivered addresses to the Consistory, and also instructed at length every Friday before the Bible Conference, which we call the congregation. He continued this course so constantly that he never failed a single time except in extreme illness. Moreover, who could recount his other common or extraordinary labors? I know of no man of our age who has had more to hear, to answer, to write, nor things of greater importance. The number and quality of his writings alone is enough to astonish any man who sees them, and still more those who read them. And what renders his labors still more astonishing is, that he had a body so feeble by nature, so debilitated by night labors and too great abstemiousness, and, what is more, subject to so many maladies, that no man who saw him could understand how he had lived so long. And yet, for all that, he never ceased to labor night and day in the work of the Lord. We entreated him to have more regard for himself; but his ordinary reply was that he was doing nothing, and that we should allow God to find him always watching, and working as he could to his latest breath."

Calvin died in 1564, eleven years after the birth of Henry of Navarre, at the age of fifty-five. For several years he was so abstemious that he had eaten but one meal a day.[A]

[Footnote A: In reference to the execution of Servetus for heresy, an event which, in the estimation of many, has seriously tarnished the reputation of Calvin, the celebrated French historian M. Mignet, in a very able dissertation, establishes the following points:

1. Servetus was not an ordinary heretic; he was a bold pantheist, and outraged the dogma of all Christian communions by saying that God, in three persons, was a Cerberus, a monster with three heads. 2. He had already been condemned

to death by the Catholic doctors at Vienne in Dauphiny. 3. The affair was judged, not by Calvin, but by the magistrates of Geneva; and if it is objected that his advice must have influenced their decision, it is necessary to recollect that the councils of the other reformed cantons of Switzerland approved the sentence with a unanimous voice. 4. It was of the utmost importance for the Reformation to separate distinctly its cause from that of such an unbeliever as Servetus. The Catholic Church, which in our day accuses Calvin of having participated in his condemnation, much more would have accused him, in the sixteenth century, with having solicited his acquittal.]

At this time the overwhelming majority of the inhabitants of France were Catholics--it has generally been estimated a hundred to one; but the doctrines of the reformers gained ground until, toward the close of the century, about the time of the Massacre of St. Bartholomew, the Protestants composed about one sixth of the population.

The storm of persecution which fell upon them was so terrible that they were compelled to protect themselves by force of arms. Gradually they gained the ascendency in several cities, which they fortified, and where they protected refugees from the persecution which had driven them from the cities where the Catholics predominated. Such was the deplorable condition of France at the time of which we write.

In the little kingdom of Navarre, which was but about one third as large as the State of Massachusetts, and which, since its dismemberment, contained less than three hundred thousand inhabitants, nearly every individual was a Protestant. Antony of Bourbon, who had married the queen, was a Frenchman. With him, as with many others in that day, religion was merely a badge of party politics. Antony spent much of his time in the voluptuous court of France, and as he was, of course, solicitous for popularity there, he espoused the Catholic side of the controversy.

Jeanne d'Albret was energetically a Protestant. Apparently, her faith was founded in deep religious conviction. When Catharine of Medici advised her to follow her husband into the Catholic Church, she replied with firmness,

"Madam, sooner than ever go to mass, if I had my kingdom and my son both in my hands, I would hurl them to the bottom of the sea before they should change my purpose."

Jeanne had been married to Antony merely as a matter of state policy. There was nothing in his character to win a noble woman's love. With no social or religious sympathies, they lived together for a time in a state of respectful indifference; but the court of Navarre was too quiet and religious to satisfy the taste of the voluptuous Parisian. He consequently spent most of his time enjoying the gayeties of the metropolis of France. A separation, mutually and amicably agreed upon, was the result.

Antony conveyed with him to Paris his son Henry, and there took up his residence. Amidst the changes and the fluctuations of the ever-agitated metropolis, he eagerly watched for opportunities to advance his own fame and fortune. As Jeanne took leave of her beloved child, she embraced him tenderly, and with tears entreated him never to abandon the faith in which he had been educated.

Jeanne d'Albret, with her little daughter, remained in the less splendid but more moral and refined metropolis of her paternal domain. A mother's solicitude and prayers, however, followed her son. Antony consented to retain as a tutor for Henry the wise and learned La Gaucherie, who was himself strongly attached to the reformed religion.

The inflexibility of Jeanne d'Albret, and the refuge she ever cheerfully afforded to the persecuted Protestants, quite enraged the Pope. As a measure of intimidation, he at one time summoned her as a heretic to appear before the Inquisition within six months, under penalty of losing her crown and her possessions. Jeanne, unawed by the threat, appealed to the monarchs of Europe for protection. None were disposed in that age to encourage such arrogant claims, and Pope Pius VI. was compelled to moderate his haughty tone. A plot, however, was then formed to seize her and her children, and hand them over to the "tender mercies" of the Spanish Inquisition. But this plot also failed.

In Paris itself there were many bold Protestant nobles who, with arms at their side, and stout retainers around them, kept personal persecution at bay. They were generally men of commanding character, of intelligence and integrity. The new religion, throughout the country, was manifestly growing fast in strength, and at times, even in the saloons of the palace, the rival parties were pretty nearly balanced. Although, throughout the kingdom of France, the Catholics were vastly more numerous than the Protestants, yet as England and much of Germany had warmly espoused the cause of the reformers, it was perhaps difficult to decide which party, on the whole, in Europe, was the strongest. Nobles and princes of the highest rank were, in all parts of Europe, ranged under either banner. In the two factions thus contending for dominion, there were, of course, some who were not much influenced by conscientious considerations, but who were merely struggling for political power.

When Henry first arrived in Paris, Catharine kept a constant watch over his words and his actions. She spared no possible efforts to bring him under her entire control. Efforts were made to lead his teacher to check his enthusiasm for lofty exploits, and to surrender him to the claims of frivolous amusement. This detestable queen presented before the impassioned young man all the blandishments of female beauty, that she might betray him to licentious indulgence. In some of these infamous arts she was but too successful.

Catharine, in her ambitious projects, was often undecided as to which cause she should espouse and which party she should call to her aid. At one time she would favor the Protestants, and again the Catholics. At about this time she suddenly turned to the Protestants, and courted them so decidedly as greatly to alarm and exasperate the Catholics. Some of the Catholic nobles formed a conspiracy, and seized Catharine and her son at the palace of Fontainebleau, and held them both as captives. The proud queen was almost frantic with indignation at the insult.

The Protestants, conscious that the conspiracy was aimed against them, rallied for the defense of the queen. The Catholics all over the kingdom sprang to arms. A bloody civil war ensued. Nearly all Europe was drawn into the conflict. Germany and England came with eager armies to the aid of the Protestants. Catharine hated the proud and haughty Elizabeth, England's domineering queen, and was very jealous of her fame and power. She resolved that she would not be indebted to her ambitious rival for aid. She therefore, most strangely, threw herself into the arms of the *Catholics*, and ardently espoused their cause. The Protestants soon found her, with all the energy of her powerful mind, heading their foes. France was deluged in blood.

A large number of Protestants threw themselves into Rouen. Antony of Bourbon headed an army of the Catholics to besiege the city. A ball struck him, and he fell senseless to the ground. His attendants placed him, covered with blood, in a carriage, to convey him to a hospital. While in the carriage and jostling over the rough ground, and as the thunders of the cannonade were pealing in his ears, the spirit of the blood-stained soldier ascended to the tribunal of the God of Peace. Henry was now left fatherless, and subject entirely to the control of his mother, whom he most tenderly loved, and whose views, as one of the most prominent leaders of the Protestant party, he was

KARTINDO PUBLISHING HOUSE (Kartindo.Com)

strongly inclined to espouse.

The sanguinary conflict still raged with unabated violence throughout the whole kingdom, arming brother against brother, friend against friend. Churches were sacked and destroyed; vast extents of country were almost depopulated; cities were surrendered to pillage, and atrocities innumerable perpetrated, from which it would seem that even fiends would revolt. France was filled with smouldering ruins; and the wailing cry of widows and of orphans, thus made by the wrath of man, ascended from every plain and every hill-side to the ear of that God who has said, "Thou shalt love thy neighbor as thyself."

At last both parties were weary of the horrid strife. The Catholics were struggling to extirpate what they deemed ruinous heresy from the kingdom. The Protestants were repelling the assault, and contending, not for general liberty of conscience, but that their doctrines *were true*, and *therefore* should be sustained. Terms of accommodation were proposed, and the Catholics made the great concession, as they regarded it, of allowing the Protestants to conduct public worship *outside of the walls of towns*. The Protestants accepted these terms, and sheathed the sword; but many of the more fanatic Catholics were greatly enraged at this toleration. The Guises, the most arrogant family of nobles the world has ever known, retired from Paris in indignation, declaring that they would not witness such a triumph of heresy. The decree which granted this poor boon was the famous edict of January, 1562, issued from St. Germain. But such a peace as this could only be a truce caused by exhaustion. Deep-seated animosity still rankled in the bosom of both parties; and, notwithstanding all the woes which desolating wars had engendered, the spirit of religious intolerance was eager again to grasp the weapons of deadly strife.

During the sixteenth century the doctrine of religious toleration was recognized by no one. That great truth had not then even dawned upon the world. The noble toleration so earnestly advocated by Bayle and Locke a century later, was almost a new revelation to the human mind; but in the sixteenth century it would have been regarded as impious, and rebellion against God to have affirmed that *error* was not to be pursued and punished. The reformers did not advocate the view that a man had a right to believe what he pleased, and to disseminate that belief. They only declared that they were bound, at all hazards, to believe the *truth;* that the views which they cherished were *true*, and that *therefore* they should be protected in them. They appealed to the Bible, and challenged their adversaries to meet them there. Our fathers must not be condemned for not being in advance of the age in which they lived. That toleration which allows a man to adopt, without any civil disabilities, any mode

KARTINDO PUBLISHING HOUSE (Kartindo.Com)

of worship that does not disturb the peace of society, exists, as we believe, only in the United States. Even in England Dissenters are excluded from many privileges. Throughout the whole of Catholic Europe no religious toleration is recognized. The Emperor Napoleon, during his reign, established the most perfect freedom of conscience in every government his influence could control. His downfall re-established through Europe the dominion of intolerance.

The Reformation, in contending for the right of private judgment in contradiction to the claims of councils, maintained a principle which necessarily involved the freedom of conscience. This was not then perceived; but time developed the truth. The Reformation became, in reality, the mother of all religious liberty.

KARTINDO PUBLISHING HOUSE (Kartindo.Com)

CHAPTER II

CIVIL WAR

1565-1568

Henry but little acquainted with his parents.--Indecision of Henry.--Hypocrisy of Catharine.--She desires to save Henry.--A significant reply.--Indications of future greatness.--The prophecy.--Visit of Catharine.--Endeavors of Catharine to influence the young prince.--The return visit.--Obstacles to the departure.--The stratagem.--Its success.--Home again.--Description of the prince.--Evil effects of dissolute society.--Influence of Jeanne d'Albret.--Catharine's deity.--Principle of Jeanne d'Albret.--The cannon the missionary.--Devastation.--Indecision of the prince.--Arguments pro and con.--Chances of a crown.--War again.--Arrival of the Queen of Navarre.--Education of the prince.--The Prince of Condé.--Slaughter of the Protestants.--The battle.--Courage of the Prince of Condé.--The defeat.--Death of the Prince of Condé.--Retreat of the Protestants.--Fiendish barbarity.--Advice of the Pope.--Incitement to massacre.--The protectorate.

While France was thus deluged with the blood of a civil war, young Henry was busily pursuing his studies in college. He could have had but little affection for his father, for the stern soldier had passed most of his days in the tented field, and his son had hardly known him. From his mother he had long been separated; but he cherished her memory with affectionate regard, and his predilections strongly inclined him toward the faith which he knew that she had so warmly espoused. It was, however, in its political aspects that Henry mainly contemplated the question. He regarded the two sects merely as two political parties struggling for power. For some time he did not venture to commit himself openly, but, availing himself of the privilege of his youth, carefully studied the principles and the prospects of the contending factions, patiently waiting for the time to come in which he should introduce his strong arm into the conflict. Each party, aware that his parents had espoused opposite sides, and regarding him as an invaluable accession to either cause, adopted all possible allurements to win his favor.

Catharine, as unprincipled as she was ambitious, invited him to her court, lavished upon him, with queenly profusion, caresses and flattery, and enticed him with all those blandishments which might most effectually enthrall the impassioned spirit of youth. Voluptuousness, gilded with its most dazzling and deceitful enchantments, was studiously presented to his eye. The queen was all love and complaisance. She received him to her cabinet council. She affected to regard him as her chief confidant. She had already formed the design of perfidiously throwing the Protestants off their guard by professions of friendship, and then, by indiscriminate massacre, of obliterating from the kingdom every vestige of the reformed faith. The great mass of the people being Catholics, she thought that, by a simultaneous uprising all over the kingdom, the Protestants might be so generally destroyed that not enough would be left to cause her any serious embarrassments.

For many reasons Catharine wished to save Henry from the doom impending over his friends, if she could, by any means, win him to her side. She held many interviews with the highest ecclesiastics upon the subject of the contemplated massacre. At one time, when she was urging the expediency of sparing some few Protestant nobles who had been her personal friends, Henry overheard the significant reply from the Duke of Alva, "The head of a salmon is worth a hundred frogs." The young prince meditated deeply upon the import of those words. Surmising their significance, and alarmed for the safety of his mother, he dispatched a trusty messenger to communicate to her his suspicions.

His mind was now thoroughly aroused to vigilance, to careful and hourly scrutiny of the plots and counterplots which were ever forming around him. While others of his age were absorbed in the pleasures of licentiousness and gaming, to which that corrupt court was abandoned, Henry, though he had not escaped unspotted from the contamination which surrounded him, displayed, by the dignity of his demeanor and the elevation of his character, those extraordinary qualities which so remarkably distinguished him in future life, and which indicated, even then, that he was born to command. One of the grandees of the Spanish court, the Duke of Medina, after meeting him incidentally but for a few moments, remarked,

"It appears to me that this young prince is either an emperor, or is destined soon to become one."

Henry was very punctilious in regard to etiquette, and would allow no one to treat him without due respect, or to deprive him of the position to which he was entitled by his rank.

KARTINDO PUBLISHING HOUSE (Kartindo.Com)

Jeanne d'Albret, the Queen of Navarre, was now considered the most illustrious leader of the Protestant party. Catharine, the better to disguise her infamous designs, went with Henry, in great splendor, to make a friendly visit to his mother in the little Protestant court of Bearn. Catharine insidiously lavished upon Jeanne d'Albret the warmest congratulations and the most winning smiles, and omitted no courtly blandishments which could disarm the suspicions and win the confidence of the Protestant queen. The situation of Jeanne in her feeble dominion was extremely embarrassing. The Pope, in consequence of her alleged heresy, had issued against her the bull of excommunication, declaring her incapable of reigning, forbidding all good Catholics, by the peril of their own salvation, from obeying any of her commands. As her own subjects were almost all Protestants, she was in no danger of any insurrection on their part; but this decree, in that age of superstition and of profligacy, invited each neighboring power to seize upon her territory. The only safety of the queen consisted in the mutual jealousies of the rival kingdoms of France and Spain, neither of them being willing that the other should receive such an accession to its political importance.

The Queen of Navarre was not at all shaken in her faith, or influenced to change her measure, by the visit of the French court to her capital. She regarded, however, with much solicitude, the ascendency which, it appeared to her, Catharine was obtaining over the mind of her son. Catharine caressed and flattered the young Prince of Navarre in every possible way. All her blandishments were exerted to obtain a commanding influence over his mind. She endeavored unceasingly to lure him to indulgence in all forbidden pleasure, and especially to crowd upon his youthful and ardent passions all the temptations which yielding female beauty could present. After the visit of a few weeks, during which the little court of Navarre had witnessed an importation of profligacy unknown before, the Queen of France, with Henry and with her voluptuous train, returned again to Paris.

Jeanne d'Albret had seen enough of the blandishments of vice to excite her deepest maternal solicitude in view of the peril of her son. She earnestly urged his return to Navarre; but Catharine continually threw such chains of influence around him that he could not escape. At last Jeanne resolved, under the pretense of returning the visit of Catharine, to go herself to the court of France and try to recover Henry. With a small but illustrious retinue, embellished with great elegance of manners and purity of life, she arrived in Paris. The Queen of France received her with every possible mark of respect and affection, and lavished upon her entertainments, and fêtes, and gorgeous spectacles until the Queen of Navarre was almost bewildered.

KARTINDO PUBLISHING HOUSE (Kartindo.Com)

[Illustration: THE FLIGHT OF THE QUEEN OF NAVARRE.]

Whenever Jeanne proposed to return to her kingdom there was some very special celebration appointed, from which Jeanne could not, without extreme rudeness, break away. Thus again and again was Jeanne frustrated in her endeavors to leave Paris, until she found, to her surprise and chagrin, that both she and her son were prisoners, detained in captivity by bonds of the most provoking politeness. Catharine managed so adroitly that Jeanne could not enter any complaints, for the shackles which were thrown around her were those of ostensibly the most excessive kindness and the most unbounded love. It was of no avail to provoke a quarrel, for the Queen of Navarre was powerless in the heart of France.

At last she resolved to effect by stratagem that which she could not accomplish openly. One day a large party had gone out upon a hunting excursion. The Queen of Navarre made arrangements with her son, and a few of the most energetic and trustworthy gentlemen of her court, to separate themselves, as it were accidentally, when in the eagerness of the chase, from the rest of the company, and to meet at an appointed place of rendezvous. The little band, thus assembled, turned the heads of their horses toward Navarre. They drove with the utmost speed day and night, furnishing themselves with fresh relays of horses, and rested not till the clatter of the iron hoofs of the steeds were heard among the mountains of Navarre. Jeanne left a very polite note upon her table in the palace of St. Cloud, thanking Queen Catharine for all her kindness, and praying her to excuse the liberty she had taken in avoiding the pain of words of adieu. Catharine was exceedingly annoyed at their escape, but, perceiving that it was not in her power to overtake the fugitives, she submitted with as good a grace as possible.

Henry found himself thus again among his native hills. He was placed under the tuition of a gentleman who had a high appreciation of all that was poetic and beautiful. Henry, under his guidance, devoted himself with great delight to the study of polite literature, and gave free wing to an ennobled imagination as he clambered up the cliffs, and wandered over the ravines familiar to the days of his childhood. His personal appearance in 1567, when he was thirteen years of age, is thus described by a Roman Catholic gentleman who was accustomed to meet him daily in the court of Catharine.

"We have here the young Prince of Bearn. One can not help acknowledging that he is a beautiful creature. At the age of thirteen he displays all the qualities of a person of eighteen or nineteen. He is agreeable, he is civil, he is obliging.

KARTINDO PUBLISHING HOUSE (Kartindo.Com)

Others might say that as yet he does not know what he is; but, for my part, I, who study him very often, can assure you that he does know perfectly well. He demeans himself toward all the world with so easy a carriage, that people crowd round wherever he is; and he acts so nobly in every thing, that one sees clearly that he is a great prince. He enters into conversation as a highly-polished man. He speaks always to the purpose, and it is remarked that he is very well informed. I shall hate the reformed religion all my life for having carried off from us so worthy a person. Without this original sin, he would be the first after the king, and we should see him, in a short time, at the head of the armies. He gains new friends every day. He insinuates himself into all hearts with inconceivable skill. He is highly honored by the men, and no less beloved by the ladies. His face is very well formed, the nose neither too large nor too small. His eyes are very soft; his skin brown, but very smooth; and his whole features animated with such uncommon vivacity, that, if he does not make progress with the fair, it will be very extraordinary."

Henry had not escaped the natural influence of the dissolute society in the midst of which he had been educated, and manifested, on his first return to his mother, a strong passion for balls and masquerades, and all the enervating pleasures of fashionable life. His courtly and persuasive manners were so insinuating, that, without difficulty, he borrowed any sums of money he pleased, and with these borrowed treasures he fed his passion for excitement at the gaming-table.

The firm principles and high intellectual elevation of his mother roused her to the immediate and vigorous endeavor to correct all these radical defects in his character and education. She kept him, as much as possible, under her own eye. She appointed teachers of the highest mental and moral attainments to instruct him. By her conversation and example she impressed upon his mind the sentiment that it was the most distinguished honor of one born to command others to be their superior in intelligence, judgment, and self-control. The Prince of Navarre, in his mother's court at Bearn, found himself surrounded by Protestant friends and influences, and he could not but feel and admit the superior dignity and purity of these his new friends.

Catharine worshiped no deity but ambition. She was ready to adopt any measures and to plunge into any crimes which would give stability and lustre to her power. She had no religious opinions or even preferences. She espoused the cause of the Catholics because, on the whole, she deemed that party the more powerful; and then she sought the entire destruction of the Protestants, that none might be left to dispute her sway. Had the Protestants been in the

KARTINDO PUBLISHING HOUSE (Kartindo.Com)

majority, she would, with equal zeal, have given them the aid of her strong arm, and unrelentingly would have striven to crush the whole papal power.

Jeanne d'Albret, on the contrary, was in *principle* a Protestant. She was a woman of reflection, of feeling, of highly-cultivated intellect, and probably of sincere piety. She had read, with deep interest, the religious controversies of the day. She had prayed for light and guidance. She had finally and cordially adopted the Protestant faith as the truth of God. Thus guided by her sense of duty, she was exceedingly anxious that her son should be a Protestant--a Protestant Christian. In most solemn prayer she dedicated him to God's service, to defend the faith of the Reformers. In the darkness of that day, the bloody and cruel sword was almost universally recognized as the great champion of truth. Both parties appeared to think that the thunders of artillery and musketry must accompany the persuasive influence of eloquence. If it were deemed important that one hand should guide the pen of controversy, to establish the truth, it was considered no less important that the other should wield the sword to extirpate heresy. Military heroism was thought as essential as scholarship for the defense of the faith.

A truly liberal mind will find its indignation, in view of the atrocities of these religious wars, mitigated by comparison in view of the ignorance and the frailty of man. The Protestants often needlessly exasperated the Catholics by demolishing, in the hour of victory, their churches, their paintings, and their statues, and by pouring contempt upon all that was most hallowed in the Catholic heart. There was, however, this marked difference between the two parties: the leaders of the Protestants, as a general rule, did every thing in their power to check the fury of their less enlightened followers. The leaders of the Catholics, as a general rule, did every thing in their power to stimulate the fanaticism of the frenzied populace. In the first religious war the Protestant soldiers broke open and plundered the great church of Orleans. The Prince of Condé and Admiral Coligni hastened to repress the disorder. The prince pointed a musket at a soldier who had ascended a ladder to break an image, threatening to shoot him if he did not immediately desist.

"My lord," exclaimed the fanatic Protestant, "wait till I have thrown down this idol, and then, if it please you, I will die."

It is well for man that Omniscience presides at the day of judgment. "The Lord knoweth our frame; he remembereth that we are dust."

KARTINDO PUBLISHING HOUSE (Kartindo.Com)

Europe was manifestly preparing for another dreadful religious conflict. The foreboding cloud blackened the skies. The young Prince of Navarre had not yet taken his side. Both Catholics and Protestants left no exertions untried to win to their cause so important an auxiliary. Henry had warm friends in the court of Navarre and in the court of St. Cloud. He was bound by many ties to both Catholics and Protestants. Love of pleasure, of self-indulgence, of power, urged him to cast in his lot with the Catholics. Reverence for his mother inclined him to adopt the weaker party, who were struggling for purity of morals and of faith. To be popular with his subjects in his own kingdom of Navarre, he must be a Protestant. To be popular in France, to whose throne he was already casting a wistful eye, it was necessary for him to be a Catholic. He vacillated between these views of self-interest. His conscience and his heart were untouched. Both parties were aware of the magnitude of the weight he could place in either scale, while each deemed it quite uncertain which cause he would espouse. His father had died contending for the Catholic faith, and all knew that the throne of Catholic France was one of the prizes which the young Prince of Navarre had a fair chance of obtaining. His mother was the most illustrious leader of the Protestant forces on the Continent, and the crown of Henry's hereditary domain could not repose quietly upon any brow but that of a Protestant.

Such was the state of affairs when the clangor of arms again burst upon the ear of Europe. France was the arena of woe upon which the Catholics and the Protestants of England and of the Continent hurled themselves against each other. Catharine, breathing vengeance, headed the Catholic armies. Jeanne, calm yet inflexible, was recognized as at the head of the Protestant leaders, and was alike the idol of the common soldiers and of their generals. The two contending armies, after various marchings and countermarchings, met at Rochelle. The whole country around, for many leagues, was illuminated at night by the camp-fires of the hostile hosts. The Protestants, inferior in numbers, with hymns and prayers calmly awaited an attack. The Catholics, divided in council, were fearful of hazarding a decisive engagement. Day after day thus passed, with occasional skirmishes, when, one sunny morning, the sound of trumpets was heard, and the gleam of the spears and banners of an approaching host was seen on the distant hills. The joyful tidings spread through the ranks of the Protestants that the Queen of Navarre, with her son and four thousand troops, had arrived. At the head of her firm and almost invincible band she rode, calm and serene, magnificently mounted, with her proud boy by her side. As the queen and her son entered the plain, an exultant shout from the whole Protestant host seemed to rend the skies. These enthusiastic plaudits, loud, long, reiterated, sent dismay to the hearts of the Catholics.

KARTINDO PUBLISHING HOUSE (Kartindo.Com)

Jeanne presented her son to the Protestant army, and solemnly dedicated him to the defense of the Protestant faith. At the same time she published a declaration to the world that she deplored the horrors of war; that she was not contending for the oppression of others, but to secure for herself and her friends the right to worship God according to the teachings of the Bible. The young prince was placed under the charge of the most experienced generals, to guard his person from danger and to instruct him in military science. The Prince of Condé was his teacher in that terrible accomplishment in which both master and pupil have obtained such worldwide renown.

Long files of English troops, with trumpet tones, and waving banners, and heavy artillery, were seen winding their way along the streams of France, hastening to the scene of conflict. The heavy battalions of the Pope were marshaling upon all the sunny plains of Italy, and the banners of the rushing squadrons glittered from the pinnacles of the Alps, as Europe rose in arms, desolating ten thousand homes with conflagrations, and blood, and woe. Could the pen record the smouldering ruins, the desolate hearthstones, the shrieks of mortal agony, the wailings of the widow, the cry of the orphan, which thus resulted from man's inhumanity to man, the heart would sicken at the recital. The summer passed away in marches and counter-marches, in assassinations, and skirmishes, and battles. The fields of the husbandmen were trampled under the hoofs of horses. Villages were burned to the ground, and their wretched inhabitants driven out in nakedness and starvation to meet the storms of merciless winter. Noble ladies and refined and beautiful maidens fled shrieking from the pursuit of brutal and licentious soldiers. Still neither party gained any decisive victory. The storms of winter came, and beat heavily, with frost and drifting snow, upon the worn and weary hosts.

In three months ten thousand Protestants had perished. At Orleans two hundred Protestants were thrown into prison. The populace set the prison on fire, and they were all consumed.

At length the Catholic armies, having become far more numerous than the Protestant, ventured upon a general engagement. They met upon the field of Jarnac. The battle was conducted by the Reformers with a degree of fearlessness bordering on desperation. The Prince of Condé plunged into the thickest ranks of the enemy with his unfurled banner bearing the motto, "Danger is sweet for Christ and my country." Just as he commenced his desperate charge, a kick from a wounded horse fractured his leg so severely that the fragments of the bone protruded through his boot. Pointing to the mangled and helpless limb, he said to those around him, "Remember the state in which Louis of Bourbon enters the fight for Christ and his country." Immediately sounding the charge, like a whirlwind his little band plunged into the midst of their foes. For a moment the shock was irresistible, and the assailed fell like grass before the scythe of the mower. Soon, however, the undaunted band was entirely surrounded by their powerful adversaries. The Prince of Condé, with but about two hundred and fifty men, with indomitable determination sustained himself against the serried ranks of five thousand men closing up around him on every side. This was the last earthly conflict of the Prince of Condé. With his leg broken and his arm nearly severed from his body, his horse fell dead beneath him, and the prince, deluged with blood, was precipitated into the dust under the trampling hoofs of wounded and frantic chargers. His men still fought with desperation around their wounded chieftain. Of twenty-five nephews who accompanied him, fifteen were slain by his side. Soon all his defenders were cut down or dispersed. The wounded prince, an invaluable prize, was taken prisoner. Montesquieu, captain of the guards of the Duke of Anjou, came driving up, and as he saw the prisoner attracting much attention, besmeared with blood and dirt,

"Whom have we here?" he inquired.

"The Prince of Condé," was the exultant reply.

"Kill him! kill him!" exclaimed the captain, and he discharged a pistol at his head.

The ball passed through his brain, and the prince fell lifeless upon the ground. The corpse was left where it fell, and the Catholic troops pursued their foes, now flying in every direction. The Protestants retreated across a river, blew up the bridge, and protected themselves from farther assault. The next day the Duke of Anjou, the younger brother of Charles IX., and who afterward became Henry III., who was one of the leaders of the Catholic army, rode over the field of battle, to find, if possible, the body of his illustrious enemy.

"We had not rode far," says one who accompanied him, "when we perceived a great number of the dead bodies piled up in a heap, which led us to judge that this was the spot where the body of the prince was to be found: in fact, we found it there. Baron de Magnac took the corpse by the hair to lift up the face, which was turned toward the ground, and asked me if I recognized him; but, as one eye was torn out, and his face was covered with blood and dirt, I could only reply that it was certainly his height and his complexion, but farther I could not say."

They washed the bloody and mangled face, and found that it was indeed the prince. His body was carried, with infamous ribaldry, on an ass to the castle of Jarnac, and thrown contemptuously upon the ground. Several illustrious prisoners were brought to the spot and butchered in cold blood, and their corpses thrown upon that of the prince, while the soldiers passed a night of drunkenness and revelry, exulting over the remains of their dead enemies.

Such was the terrible battle of Jarnac, the first conflict which Henry witnessed. The tidings of this great victory and of the death of the illustrious Condé excited transports of joy among the Catholics. Charles IX. sent to Pope Pius V. the standards taken from the Protestants. The Pope, who affirmed that Luther was a ravenous beast, and that his doctrines were the sum of all crimes, wrote to the king a letter of congratulation. He urged him to extirpate every fibre of heresy, regardless of all entreaty, and of every tie of blood and affection. To encourage him, he cited the example of Saul exterminating the Amalekites, and assured him that all tendency to clemency was a snare of the devil.

The Catholics now considered the condition of the Protestants as desperate. The pulpits resounded with imprecations and anathemas. The Catholic priests earnestly advocated the sentiment that no faith was to be kept with heretics; that to massacre them was an action essential to the safety of the state, and which would secure the approbation of God.

But the Protestants, though defeated, were still unsubdued. The noble Admiral Coligni still remained to them; and after the disaster, Jeanne d'Albret presented herself before the troops, holding her son Henry, then fourteen years of age, by one hand, and Henry, son of the Prince de Condé, by the other, and devoted them both to the cause. The young Henry of Navarre was then proclaimed *generalissimo* of the army and *protector* of the churches. He took the following oath: "I swear to defend the Protestant religion, and to persevere in the common cause, till death or till victory has secured for all the liberty which we desire."

CHAPTER III

THE MARRIAGE

1568-1572

Emotions of Henry.--His military sagacity.--Enthusiasm inspired by Jeanne.--The failure of Catharine.--The second defeat.--The wounded friends.--The reserve force.--Misfortunes of Coligni.--His letter.--The third army.--The tide of victory changed.--The treaty of St. Germaine-en-Laye.--Perfidy of Catharine.--The court at Rochelle.--The two courts.--Marriage of Elizabeth.--The Princess Marguerite.--Effects of the connection.--A royal match.--Repugnance of Jeanne d'Albret.--Objections overcome.--Perjury of Charles IX.--Displays of friendship.--Indifference of Marguerite.--Preparations for the wedding.--Death of Jeanne.--Demonstrations of grief.--Different reports.--The King of Navarre.--Indifference.--Coligni lured to Paris.--He is remonstrated with.--The nuptial day.--The scene.--Small favors gratefully received.--Mass.--National festivities.--The tournament.--Strange representations.--Regal courtesy.--Impediments to departure.--Mission from the Pope.--The reply.

Young Henry of Navarre was but about fourteen years of age when, from one of the hills in the vicinity, he looked upon the terrible battle of Jarnac. It is reported that, young as he was, he pointed out the fatal errors which were committed by the Protestants in all the arrangements which preceded the battle.

"It is folly," he said, "to think of fighting, with forces so divided, a united army making an attack at one point."

For the security of his person, deemed so precious to the Protestants, his friends, notwithstanding his entreaties and even tears, would not allow him to expose himself to any of the perils of the conflict. As he stood upon an eminence which overlooked the field of battle, surrounded by a few faithful guards, he gazed with intense anguish upon the sanguinary scene spread out before him. He saw his friends utterly defeated, and their squadrons trampled in the dust beneath the hoofs of the Catholic cavalry.

The Protestants, without loss of time, rallied anew their forces. The Queen of

Navarre soon saw thousands of strong arms and brave hearts collecting again around her banner. Accompanied by her son, she rode through their ranks, and addressed them in words of feminine yet heroic eloquence, which roused their utmost enthusiasm. But few instances have been recorded in which human hearts have been more deeply moved than were these martial hosts by the brief sentences which dropped from the lips of this extraordinary woman. Henry, in the most solemn manner, pledged himself to consecrate all his energies to the defense of the Protestant religion. To each of the chiefs of the army the queen also presented a gold medal, suspended from a golden chain, with her own name and that of her son impressed upon one side, and on the other the words "Certain peace, complete victory, or honorable death." The enthusiasm of the army was raised to the highest pitch, and the heroic queen became the object almost of the adoration of her soldiers.

Catharine, seeing the wonderful enthusiasm with which the Protestant troops were inspired by the presence of the Queen of Navarre, visited the head-quarters of her own army, hoping that she might also enkindle similar ardor. Accompanied by a magnificent retinue of her brilliantly-accoutred generals, she swept, like a gorgeous vision, before her troops. She lavished presents upon her officers, and in high-sounding phrase harangued the soldiers; but there was not a private in the ranks who did not know that she was a wicked and a polluted woman. She had talent, but no soul. All her efforts were unavailing to evoke one single electric spark of emotion. She had sense enough to perceive her signal failure and to feel its mortification. No one either loved or respected Catharine. Thousands hated her, yet, conscious of her power, either courting her smiles or dreading her frown, they often bowed before her in adulation.

The two armies were soon facing each other upon the field of battle. It was the third of October, 1569. More than fifty thousand combatants met upon the plains of Moncontour. All generalship seemed to be ignored as the exasperated adversaries rushed upon each other in a headlong fight. The Protestants, outnumbered, were awfully defeated. Out of twenty-five thousand combatants whom they led into the field, but eight thousand could be rallied around their retreating banner after a fight of but three quarters of an hour. All their cannon, baggage, and munitions of war were lost. No mercy was granted to the vanquished.

Coligni, at the very commencement of the battle, was struck by a bullet which shattered his jaw. The gushing blood under his helmet choked him, and they bore him upon a litter from the field. As they were carrying the wounded admiral along, they overtook another litter upon which was stretched

L'Estrange, the bosom friend of the admiral, also desperately wounded. L'Estrange, forgetting himself, gazed for a moment with tearful eyes upon the noble Coligni, and then gently said, "It is sweet to trust in God." Coligni, unable to speak, could only *look* a reply. Thus the two wounded friends parted. Coligni afterward remarked that these few words were a cordial to his spirit, inspiring him with resolution and hope.

Henry of Navarre, and his cousin, Henry of Condé, son of the prince who fell at the battle of Jarnac, from a neighboring eminence witnessed this scene of defeat and of awful carnage. The admiral, unwilling to expose to danger lives so precious to their cause, had stationed them there with a reserve of four thousand men under the command of Louis of Nassau. When Henry saw the Protestants giving way, he implored Louis that they should hasten with the reserve to the protection of their friends; but Louis, with military rigor, awaited the commands of the admiral. "We lose our advantage, then," exclaimed the prince, "and consequently the battle."

The most awful of earthly calamities seemed now to fall like an avalanche upon Coligni, the noble Huguenot chieftain. His beloved brother was slain. Bands of wretches had burned down his castle and laid waste his estates. The Parliament of Paris, composed of zealous Catholics, had declared him guilty of high treason, and offered fifty thousand crowns to whoever would deliver him up, dead or alive. The Pope declared to all Europe that he was a "detestable, infamous, execrable man, if, indeed, he even merited the name of man." His army was defeated, his friends cut to pieces, and he himself was grievously wounded, and was lying upon a couch in great anguish. Under these circumstances, thirteen days after receiving his wound, he thus wrote to his children:

"We should not repose on earthly possessions. Let us place our hope beyond the earth, and acquire other treasures than those which we see with our eyes and touch with our hands. We must follow Jesus our leader, who has gone before us. Men have ravished us of what they could. If such is the will of God, we shall be happy and our condition good, since we endure this loss from no wrong you have done those who have brought it to you, but solely for the hate they have borne me because God was pleased to direct me to assist his Church. For the present, it is enough to admonish and conjure you, in the name of God, to persevere courageously in the study of virtue."

In the course of a few weeks Coligni rose from his bed, and the Catholics were amazed to find him at the head of a third army. The indomitable Queen of

Navarre, with the calm energy which ever signalized her character, had rallied the fugitives around her, and had reanimated their waning courage by her own invincible spirit. Nobles and peasants from all the mountains of Bearn, and from every province in France, thronged to the Protestant camp. Conflict after conflict ensued. The tide of victory now turned in favor of the Reformers. Henry, absolutely refusing any longer to retire from the perils of the field, engaged with the utmost coolness, judgment, and yet impetuosity in all the toils and dangers of the battle. The Protestant cause gained strength. The Catholics were disheartened. Even Catharine became convinced that the extermination of the Protestants by force was no longer possible. So once more they offered conditions of peace, which were promptly accepted. These terms, which were signed at St. Germaine-en-Laye the 8th of August, 1570, were more favorable than the preceding. The Protestants were allowed liberty of worship in all the places then in their possession. They were also allowed public worship in two towns in each province of the kingdom. They were permitted to reside any where without molestation, and were declared *eligible* to any public office.

Coligni, mourning over the untold evils and miseries of war, with alacrity accepted these conditions. "Sooner than fall back into these disturbances," said he, "I would choose to die a thousand deaths, and be dragged through the streets of Paris."

The queen, however, and her advisers were guilty of the most extreme perfidy in this truce. It was merely their object to induce the foreign troops who had come to the aid of the allies to leave the kingdom, that they might then exterminate the Protestants by a general massacre. Catharine decided to accomplish by the dagger of the assassin that which she had in vain attempted to accomplish on the field of battle. This peace was but the first act in the awful tragedy of St. Bartholomew.

Peace being thus apparently restored, the young Prince of Navarre now returned to his hereditary domains and visited its various provinces, where he was received with the most lively demonstrations of affection. Various circumstances, however, indicated to the Protestant leaders that some mysterious and treacherous plot was forming for their destruction. The Protestant gentlemen absented themselves, consequently, from the court of Charles IX. The king and his mother were mortified by these evidences that their perfidy was suspected.

Jeanne, with her son, after visiting her subjects in all parts of her own dominions, went to Rochelle, where they were joined by many of the most illustrious of their friends. Large numbers gathered around them, and the court of the Queen of Navarre was virtually transferred to that place. Thus there were two rival courts, side by side, in the same kingdom. Catharine, with her courtiers, exhibited boundless luxury and voluptuousness at Paris. Jeanne d'Albret, at Rochelle, embellished her court with all that was noble in intellect, elegant in manners, and pure in morals. Catharine and her submissive son Charles IX. left nothing untried to lure the Protestants into a false security. Jeanne scrupulously requited the courtesies she received from Catharine, though she regarded with much suspicion the adulation and the sycophancy of her proud hostess.

The young King of France, Charles IX., who was of about the same age with Henry, and who had been his companion and playmate in childhood, was now married to Elizabeth, the daughter of the Emperor Maximilian II. of Austria. Their nuptials were celebrated with all the ostentatious pomp which the luxury of the times and the opulence of the French monarchy could furnish. In these rejoicings the courts of France and Navarre participated with the semblance of the most heartfelt cordiality. Protestants and Catholics, pretending to forget that they had recently encountered each other with fiendlike fury in fields of blood, mingled gayly in these festivities, and vied with each other in the exchange of courtly greetings and polished flatteries. Catharine and Charles IX. lavished, with the utmost profusion, their commendations and attentions upon the young Prince of Navarre, and left no arts of dissimulation unessayed which might disarm the fears and win the confidence of their victims.

The queen mother, with caressing fondness, declared that Henry must be her son. She would confer upon him Marguerite, her youngest daughter. This princess had now become a young lady, beautiful in the extreme, and highly accomplished in all those graces which can kindle the fires and feed the flames of passion; but she was also as devoid of principle as any male libertine who contaminated by his presence a court whose very atmosphere was corruption. Many persons of royal blood had most earnestly sought the hand of this princess, for an alliance with the royal family of France was an honor which the proudest sovereigns might covet. Such a connection, in its political aspects, was every thing Henry could desire. It would vastly augment the consideration and the power of the young prince, and would bring him a long step nearer to the throne of France. The Protestants were all intensely interested in this match, as it would invest one, destined soon to become their most prominent leader, with new ability to defend their rights and to advocate their cause. It is a singular illustration of the hopeless corruption of the times, that the notorious profligacy of Marguerite seems to have been considered, even by Henry himself, as no obstacle to the union.

KARTINDO PUBLISHING HOUSE (Kartindo.Com)

A royal marriage is ordinarily but a matter of state policy. Upon the cold and icy eminence of kingly life the flowers of sympathy and affection rarely bloom. Henry, without hesitation, acquiesced in the expediency of this nuptial alliance. He regarded it as manifestly a very politic partnership, and did not concern himself in the least about the agreeable or disagreeable qualities of his contemplated spouse. He had no idea of making her his companion, much less his friend. She was to be merely his *wife*.

Jeanne d'Albret, however, a woman of sincere piety, and in whose bosom all noble thoughts were nurtured, cherished many misgivings. Her Protestant principles caused her to shrink from the espousals of her son with a Roman Catholic. Her religious scruples, and the spotless purity of her character, aroused the most lively emotions of repugnance in view of her son's connection with one who had not even the modesty to conceal her vices. State considerations, however, finally prevailed, and Jeanne, waiving her objections, consented to the marriage. She yielded, however, with the greatest reluctance, to the unceasing importunities of her friends. They urged that this marriage would unite the two parties in a solid peace, and thus protect the Protestants from persecution, and rescue France from unutterable woe. Even the Admiral Coligni was deceived. But the result proved, in this case as in every other, that *it is never safe to do evil that good may come*. If any fact is established under the government of God, it is this.

The Queen of Navarre, in her extreme repugnance to this match, remarked,

"I would choose to descend to the condition of the poorest damsel in France rather than sacrifice to the grandeur of my family my own soul and that of my son."

With consummate perjury, Charles IX. declared, "I give my sister in marriage, not only to the Prince of Navarre, but, as it were, to the whole Protestant party. This will be the strongest and closest bond for the maintenance of peace between my subjects, and a sure evidence of my good-will toward the Protestants."

Thus influenced, this noble woman consented to the union. She then went to Blois to meet Catharine and the king. They received her with exuberant displays of love. The foolish king quite overacted his part, calling her "his great aunt, his all, his best beloved." As the Queen of Navarre retired for the night, Charles said to Catharine, laughing,

"Well, mother, what do you think of it? Do I play my little part well?"

"Yes," said Catharine, encouragingly, "very well; but it is of no use unless it continues."

"Allow me to go on," said the king, "and you will see that I shall ensnare them."

The young Princess Marguerite, heartless, proud, and petulant, received the cold addresses of Henry with still more chilling indifference. She refused to make even the slightest concessions to his religious views, and, though she made no objection to the decidedly politic partnership, she very ostentatiously displayed her utter disregard for Henry and his friends. The haughty and dissolute beauty was piqued by the reluctance which Jeanne had manifested to an alliance which Marguerite thought should have been regarded as the very highest of all earthly honors. Preparations were, however, made for the marriage ceremony, which was to be performed in the French capital with unexampled splendor. The most distinguished gentlemen of the Protestant party, nobles, statesmen, warriors, from all parts of the realm, were invited to the metropolis, to add lustre to the festivities by their presence. Many, however, of the wisest counselors of the Queen of Navarre, deeply impressed with the conviction of the utter perfidy of Catharine, and apprehending some deep-laid plot, remonstrated against the acceptance of the invitations, presaging that, "if the wedding were celebrated in Paris, the liveries would be very crimson."

Jeanne, solicited by the most pressing letters from Catharine and her son Charles IX., and urged by her courtiers, who were eager to share the renowned pleasures of the French metropolis, proceeded to Paris. She had hardly entered the sumptuous lodgings provided for her in the court of Catharine, when she was seized with a violent fever, which raged in her veins nine days, and then she died. In death she manifested the same faith and fortitude which had embellished her life. Not a murmur or a groan escaped her lips in the most violent paroxysms of pain. She had no desire to live except from maternal solicitude for her children, Henry and Catharine.

"But God," said she, "will be their father and protector, as he has been mine in my greatest afflictions. I confide them to his providence."

She died in June, 1572, in the forty-fourth year of her age. Catharine exhibited the most ostentatious and extravagant demonstrations of grief. Charles gave utterance to loud and poignant lamentations, and ordered a surgeon to examine the body, that the cause of her death might be ascertained. Notwithstanding these efforts to allay suspicion, the report spread like wildfire through all the departments of France, and all the Protestant countries of Europe, that the queen had been perfidiously poisoned by Catharine. The Protestant writers of the time assert that she fell a victim to poison communicated by a pair of perfumed gloves. The Catholics as confidently affirm that she died of a natural disease. The truth can now never be known till the secrets of all hearts shall be revealed at the judgment day.

Henry, with his retinue, was slowly traveling toward Paris, unconscious of his mother's sickness, when the unexpected tidings arrived of her death. It is difficult to imagine what must have been the precise nature of the emotions of an ambitious young man in such an event, who ardently loved both his mother and the crown which she wore, as by the loss of the one he gained the other. The cloud of his grief was embellished with the gilded edgings of joy. The Prince of Bearn now assumed the title and the style of the King of Navarre, and honored the memory of his noble mother with every manifestation of regret and veneration. This melancholy event caused the postponement of the marriage ceremony for a short time, as it was not deemed decorous that epithalamiums should be shouted and requiems chanted from the same lips in the same hour. The knell tolling the burial of the dead would not blend harmoniously with the joyous peals of the marriage bell. Henry was not at all annoyed by this delay, for no impatient ardor urged him to his nuptials. Marguerite, annoyed by the opposition which Henry's mother had expressed in regard to the alliance, and vexed by the utter indifference which her betrothed manifested toward her person, indulged in all the wayward humors of a worse than spoiled child. She studiously displayed her utter disregard for Henry, which manifestations, with the most provoking indifference, he did not seem even to notice.

During this short interval the Protestant nobles continued to flock to Paris, that they might honor with their presence the marriage of the young chief. The Admiral Coligni was, by very special exertions on the part of Catharine and Charles, lured to the metropolis. He had received anonymous letters warning him of his danger. Many of his more prudent friends openly remonstrated against his placing himself in the power of the perfidious queen. Coligni, however, was strongly attached to Henry, and, in defiance of all these warnings, he resolved to attend his nuptials. "I confide," said he, "in the sacred word of his majesty."

Upon his arrival in the metropolis, Catharine and Charles lavished upon him the most unbounded manifestations of regard. The king, embracing the admiral, exclaimed, "This is the happiest day of my life." Very soon one of the admiral's friends called upon him to take leave, saying that he was immediately about to retire into the country. When asked by the admiral the cause of his unexpected departure, he replied, "I go because they caress you too much, and I would rather save myself with fools than perish with sages."

At length the nuptial day arrived. It was the seventeenth of August, 1572. Paris had laid aside its mourning weeds, and a gay and brilliant carnival succeeded its dismal days of gloom. Protestants and Catholics, of highest name and note, from every part of Europe, who had met in the dreadful encounters of a hundred fields of blood, now mingled in apparent fraternity with the glittering throng, all interchanging smiles and congratulations. The unimpassioned bridegroom led his scornful bride to the church of Notre Dame. Before the massive portals of this renowned edifice, and under the shadow of its venerable towers, a magnificent platform had been reared, canopied with the most gorgeous tapestry. Hundreds of thousands thronged the surrounding amphitheatre, swarming at the windows, crowding the balconies, and clustered upon the house-tops, to witness the imposing ceremony. The gentle breeze breathing over the multitude was laden with the perfume of flowers. Banners, and pennants, and ribbons of every varied hue waved in the air, or hung in gay festoons from window to window, and from roof to roof. Upon that conspicuous platform, in the presence of all the highest nobility of France, and of the most illustrious representatives of every court of Europe, Henry received the hand of the haughty princess, and the nuptial oath was administered.

Marguerite, however, even in that hour, and in the presence of all those spectators, gave a ludicrous exhibition of her girlish petulance and ungoverned willfulness. When, in the progress of the ceremony, she was asked if she willingly received Henry of Bourbon for her husband, she pouted, coquettishly tossed her proud head, and was silent. The question was repeated. The spirit of Marguerite was now roused, and all the powers of Europe could not tame the shrew. She fixed her eyes defiantly upon the officiating bishop, and refusing, by look, or word, or gesture, to express the slightest assent, remained as immovable as a statue. Embarrassment and delay ensued. Her royal brother, Charles IX., fully aware of his sister's indomitable resolution, coolly walked up to the termagant at bay, and placing one hand upon her chest and the other upon the back of her head, compelled an involuntary nod. The bishop smiled and bowed, and acting upon the principle that small favors were gratefully received, proceeded with the ceremony. Such were the vows with which Henry and Marguerite were united. Such is too often *love in the palace*.

KARTINDO PUBLISHING HOUSE (Kartindo.Com)

[Illustration: THE MARRIAGE.]

The Roman Catholic wife, unaccompanied by her Protestant husband, who waited at the door with his retinue, now entered the church of Notre Dame to participate in the solemnities of the mass. The young King of Navarre then submissively received his bride and conducted her to a very magnificent dinner. Catharine and Charles IX., at this entertainment, were very specially attentive to the Protestant nobles. The weak and despicable king leaned affectionately upon the arm of the Admiral Coligni, and for a long time conversed with him with every appearance of friendship and esteem. Balls, illuminations, and pageants ensued in the evening. For many days these unnatural and chilling nuptials were celebrated with all the splendor of national festivities. Among these entertainments there was a tournament, singularly characteristic of the times, and which certainly sheds peculiar lustre either upon the humility or upon the good-nature of the Protestants.

A large area was prepared for the display of one of those barbaric passes of arms in which the rude chivalry of that day delighted. The inclosure was surrounded by all the polished intellect, rank, and beauty of France. Charles IX., with his two brothers and several of the Catholic nobility, then appeared upon one side of the arena on noble war-horses gorgeously caparisoned, and threw down the gauntlet of defiance to Henry of Navarre and his Protestant retinue, who, similarly mounted and accoutred, awaited the challenge upon the opposite side.

The portion of the inclosure in which the Catholics appeared was decorated to represent heaven. Birds of Paradise displayed their gorgeous plumage, and the air was vocal with the melody of trilling songsters. Beauty displayed its charms arrayed in celestial robes, and ambrosial odors lulled the senses in luxurious indulgence. All the resources of wealth and art were lavished to create a vision of the home of the blessed.

The Protestants, in the opposite extreme of the arena, were seen emerging from the desolation, the gloom, and the sulphurous canopy of hell. The two parties, from their antagonistic realms, rushed to the encounter, the fiends of darkness battling with the angels of light. Gradually the Catholics, in accordance with previous arrangements, drove back the Protestants toward their grim abodes, when suddenly numerous demons appeared rushing from the dungeons of the infernal regions, who, with cloven hoofs, and satanic weapons, and chains forged in penal fires, seized upon the Protestants and dragged them to the blackness of darkness from whence they had emerged. Plaudits loud and long greeted this discomfiture of the Protestants by the infernal powers.

But suddenly the scene is changed. A winged Cupid appears, the representative of the pious and amiable bride Marguerite. The demons fly in dismay before the irresistible boy. Fearlessly this emissary of love penetrates the realms of despair. The Protestants, by this agency, are liberated from their thralldom, and conducted in triumph to the Elysium of the Catholics. A more curious display of regal courtesy history has not recorded. And this was in Paris!

Immediately after the marriage, the Admiral Coligni was anxious to obtain permission to leave the city. His devout spirit found no enjoyment in the gayeties of the metropolis, and he was deeply disgusted with the unveiled licentiousness which he witnessed every where around him. Day after day, however, impediments were placed in the way of his departure, and it was not until three days after the marriage festivities that he succeeded in obtaining an audience with Charles. He accompanied Charles to the racket-court, where the young monarch was accustomed to spend much of his time, and there bidding him adieu, left him to his amusements, and took his way on foot toward his lodgings.

The Pope, not aware of the treachery which was contemplated, was much displeased in view of the apparently friendly relations which had thus suddenly sprung up between the Catholics and the Protestants. He was exceedingly perplexed by the marriage, and at last sent a legate to expostulate with the French king. Charles IX. was exceedingly embarrassed how to frame a reply. He wished to convince the legate of his entire devotion to the Papal Church, and, at the same time, he did not dare to betray his intentions; for the detection of the conspiracy would not only frustrate all his plans, but would load him with ignominy, and vastly augment the power of his enemies.

"I do devoutly wish," Charles replied, "that I could tell you all; but you and the Pope shall soon know how beneficial this marriage shall prove to the interests of religion. Take my word for it, in a little time the holy father shall have reason to praise my designs, my piety, and my zeal in behalf of the faith."

CHAPTER IV

PREPARATIONS FOR MASSACRE

1572

The attempted assassination of Coligni.--Escape of the assassin.--Arrival of Henry.--Christian submission of Coligni.--Indignation of Henry.--Artifice of Catharine and Charles.--Perplexity of the Protestants.--Secret preparations.--Feeble condition of the Protestants.--The visit.--The secret council.--Preparations to arm the citizens.--Directions for the massacre.--Signals.--Feast at the Louvre.--Embarrassment of Henry.--The Duke of Lorraine.--His hatred toward the Protestants.--The assassin's revenge.--Anxiety of the Duchess of Lorraine.--Scene in Henry's chamber.--Rumors of trouble.--Assembling for work.--Alarm in the metropolis.--Inflexibility of Catharine.--The faltering of Charles.--Nerved for the work.--The knell of death.--"Vive Dieu et le roi!"

As the Admiral Coligni was quietly passing through the streets from his interview with Charles at the Louvre to his residence, in preparation for his departure, accompanied by twelve or fifteen of his personal friends, a letter was placed in his hands. He opened it, and began to read as he walked slowly along. Just as he was turning a corner of the street, a musket was discharged from the window of an adjoining house, and two balls struck him. One cut off a finger of his right hand, and the other entered his left arm. The admiral, inured to scenes of danger, manifested not the slightest agitation or alarm. He calmly pointed out to his friends the house from which the gun had been discharged, and his attendants rushed forward and broke open the door. The assassin, however, escaped through a back window, and, mounting a fleet horse stationed there, and which was subsequently proved to have belonged to a nephew of the king, avoided arrest. It was clearly proved in the investigations which immediately ensued that the assassin was in connivance with some of the most prominent Catholics of the realm. The Duke of Guise and Catharine were clearly implicated.

Messengers were immediately dispatched to inform the king of the crime which had been perpetrated. Charles was still playing in the tennis-court. Casting away his racket, he exclaimed, with every appearance of indignation, "Shall I never be at peace?"

The wounded admiral was conveyed to his lodgings. The surgeons of the court, the ministers of the Protestant Church, and the most illustrious princes and nobles of the admiral's party hastened to the couch of the sufferer. Henry of Navarre was one of the first that arrived, and he was deeply moved as he bent over his revered and much-loved friend. The intrepid and noble old man seemed perfectly calm and composed, reposing unfailing trust in God.

"My friends," said he, "why do you weep? For myself, I deem it an honor to have received these wounds for the name of God. Pray him to strengthen me."

Henry proceeded from the bedside of the admiral to the Louvre. He found Charles and Catharine there, surrounded by many of the nobles of their court. In indignant terms Henry reproached both mother and son with the atrocity of the crime which had been committed, and demanded immediate permission to retire from Paris, asserting that neither he nor his friends could any longer remain in the capital in safety. The king and his mother vied with each other in noisy, voluble, and even blasphemous declarations of their utter abhorrence of the deed; but all the oaths of Charles and all the vociferations of Catharine did but strengthen the conviction of the Protestants that they both were implicated in this plot of assassination. Catharine and Charles, feigning the deepest interest in the fate of their wounded guest, hastened to his sick-chamber with every possible assurance of their distress and sympathy. Charles expressed the utmost indignation at the murderous attempt, and declared, with those oaths which are common to vulgar minds, that he would take the most terrible vengeance upon the perpetrators as soon as he could discover them.

"To discover them can not be difficult," coolly replied the admiral.

Henry of Navarre, overwhelmed with indignation and sorrow, was greatly alarmed in view of the toils in which he found himself and his friends hopelessly involved. The Protestants, who had been thus lured to Paris, unarmed and helpless, were panic-stricken by these indications of relentless perfidy. They immediately made preparations to escape from the city. Henry, bewildered by rumors of plots and perils, hesitated whether to retire from the capital with his friends in a body, taking the admiral with them, or more secretly to endeavor to effect an escape.

But Catharine and Charles, the moment for action having not quite arrived, were unwearied in their exertions to allay this excitement and soothe these alarms. They became renewedly clamorous in their expressions of grief and indignation in view of the assault upon the admiral. The king placed a strong guard around the house where the wounded nobleman lay, ostensibly for the purpose of protecting him from any popular outbreak, but in reality, as it subsequently appeared, to guard against his escape through the intervention of his friends. He also, with consummate perfidy, urged the Protestants in the city to occupy quarters near together, that, in case of trouble, they might more easily be protected by him, and might more effectually aid one another. His real object, however, was to assemble them in more convenient proximity for the slaughter to which they were doomed. The Protestants were in the deepest perplexity. They were not sure but that all their apprehensions were groundless; and yet they knew not but that in the next hour some fearful battery would be unmasked for their destruction. They were unarmed, unorganized, and unable to make any preparation to meet an unknown danger. Catharine, whose depraved yet imperious spirit was guiding with such consummate duplicity all this enginery of intrigue, hourly administered the stimulus of her own stern will to sustain the faltering purpose of her equally depraved but fickle-minded and imbecile son.

Some circumstances seem to indicate that Charles was not an accomplice with his mother in the attempt upon the life of the admiral. She said to her son, "Notwithstanding all your protestations, the deed will certainly be laid to your charge. Civil war will again be enkindled. The chiefs of the Protestants are now all in Paris. You had better gain the victory at once here than incur the hazard of a new campaign."

"Well, then," said Charles, petulantly, "since you approve the murder of the admiral, I am content. But let all the Huguenots also fall, that there may not be one left to reproach me."

It was on Friday, the 22d of August, that the bullets of the assassin wounded Coligni. The next day Henry called again, with his bride, to visit his friend, whose finger had been amputated, and who was suffering extreme pain from the wound in his arm. Marguerite had but few sympathies with the scenes which are to be witnessed in the chamber of sickness. She did not conceal her impatience, but, after a few commonplace phrases of condolence with her husband's bosom friend, she hastened away, leaving Henry to perform alone the offices of friendly sympathy.

While the young King of Navarre was thus sitting at the bedside of the admiral, recounting to him the assurances of faith and honor given by Catharine and her son, the question was then under discussion, in secret council, at the palace, by this very Catharine and Charles, whether Henry, the husband of the daughter of the one and of the sister of the other, should be included with the rest of the Protestants in the massacre which they were plotting. Charles manifested some reluctance thus treacherously to take the life of his early playmate and friend, his brother-in-law, and his invited guest. It was, after much deliberation, decided to protect him from the general slaughter to which his friends were destined.

The king sent for some of the leading officers of his troops, and commanded them immediately, but secretly, to send his agents through every section of the city, to arm the Roman Catholic citizens, and assemble them, at midnight, in front of the Hotel de Ville.

The energetic Duke of Guise, who had acquired much notoriety by the sanguinary spirit with which he had persecuted the Protestants, was to take the lead of the carnage. To prevent mistakes in the confusion of the night, he had issued secret orders for all the Catholics "to wear a white cross on the hat, and to bind a piece of white cloth around the arm." In the darkest hour of the night, when all the sentinels of vigilance and all the powers of resistance should be most effectually disarmed by sleep, the alarm-bell, from the tower of the Palace of Justice, was to toll the signal for the indiscriminate massacre of the Protestants. The bullet and the dagger were to be every where employed, and men, women, and children were to be cut down without mercy. With a very few individual exceptions, none were to be left to avenge the deed. Large bodies of troops, who hated the Protestants with that implacable bitterness which the most sanguinary wars of many years had engendered, had been called into the city, and they, familiar with deeds of blood, were to commence the slaughter. All good citizens were enjoined, as they loved their Savior, to aid in the extermination of the enemies of the Church of Rome. Thus, it was declared, God would be glorified and the best interests of man promoted. The spirit of the age was in harmony with the act, and it can not be doubted that there were those who had been so instructed by their spiritual guides that they truly believed that by this sacrifice they were doing God service.

The conspiracy extended throughout all the provinces of France. The storm was to burst, at the same moment, upon the unsuspecting victims in every city and village of the kingdom. Beacon-fires, with their lurid midnight glare, were to flash the tidings from mountain to mountain. The peal of alarm was to ring along from steeple to steeple, from city to hamlet, from valley to hill-side, till the whole Catholic population should be aroused to obliterate every vestige of Protestantism from the land.

While Catharine and Charles were arranging all the details of this deed of infamy, even to the very last moment they maintained with the Protestants the appearance of the most cordial friendship. They lavished caresses upon the Protestant generals and nobles. The very day preceding the night when the massacre commenced, the king entertained, at a sumptuous feast in the Louvre, many of the most illustrious of the doomed guests. Many of the Protestant nobles were that night, by the most pressing invitations, detained in the palace to sleep. Charles appeared in a glow of amiable spirits, and amused them, till a late hour, with his pleasantries.

Henry of Navarre, however, had his suspicions very strongly aroused. Though he did not and could not imagine any thing so dreadful as a general massacre, he clearly foresaw that preparations were making for some very extraordinary event. The entire depravity of both Catharine and Charles he fully understood. But he knew not where the blow would fall, and he was extremely perplexed in deciding as to the course he ought to pursue. The apartments assigned to him and his bride were in the palace of the Louvre. It would be so manifestly for his worldly interest for him to unite with the Catholic party, especially when he should see the Protestant cause hopelessly ruined, that the mother and the brother of his wife had hesitatingly concluded that it would be safe to spare his life. Many of the most conspicuous members of the court of Navarre lodged also in the capacious palace, in chambers contiguous to those which were occupied by their sovereign.

Marguerite's oldest sister had married the Duke of Lorraine, and her son, the Duke of Guise, an energetic, ambitious, unprincipled profligate, was one of the most active agents in this conspiracy. His illustrious rank, his near relationship with the king--rendering it not improbable that he might yet inherit the throne--his restless activity, and his implacable hatred of the Protestants, gave him the most prominent position as the leader of the Catholic party. He had often encountered the Admiral Coligni upon fields of battle, where all the malignity of the human heart had been aroused, and he had often been compelled to fly before the strong arm of his powerful adversary. He felt that now the hour of revenge had come, and with an assassin's despicable heart he thirsted for the blood of his noble foe. It was one of his paid agents who fired upon the admiral from the window, and, mounted upon one of the fleetest chargers of the Duke of Guise, the wretch made his escape.

The conspiracy had been kept a profound secret from Marguerite, lest she should divulge it to her husband. The Duchess of Lorraine, however, was in all their deliberations, and, fully aware of the dreadful carnage which the night was to witness, she began to feel, as the hour of midnight approached, very considerable anxiety in reference to the safety of her sister. Conscious guilt magnified her fears; and she was apprehensive lest the Protestants, when they should first awake to the treachery which surrounded them, would rush to the chamber of their king to protect him, and would wreak their vengeance upon his Catholic spouse. She did not dare to communicate to her sister the cause of her alarm; and yet, when Marguerite, about 11 o'clock, arose to retire, she importuned her sister, even with tears, not to occupy the same apartment with her husband that night, but to sleep in her own private chamber. Catharine sharply reproved the Duchess of Lorraine for her imprudent remonstrances, and bidding the Queen of Navarre good-night, with maternal authority directed her to repair to the room of her husband. She departed to the nuptial chamber, wondering what could be the cause of such an unwonted display of sisterly solicitude and affection.

When she entered her room, to her great surprise she found thirty or forty gentlemen assembled there. They were the friends and the supporters of Henry, who had become alarmed by the mysterious rumors which were floating from ear to ear, and by the signs of agitation, and secrecy, and strange preparation which every where met the eye. No one could imagine what danger was impending. No one knew from what quarter the storm would burst. But that some very extraordinary event was about to transpire was evident to all. It was too late to adopt any precautions for safety. The Protestants, unarmed, unorganized, and widely dispersed, could now only practice the virtue of heroic fortitude in meeting their doom, whatever that doom might be. The gentlemen in Henry's chamber did not venture to separate, and not an eye was closed in sleep. They sat together in the deepest perplexity and consternation, as the hours of the night lingered slowly along, anxiously awaiting the developments with which the moments seemed to be fraught.

In the mean time, aided by the gloom of a starless night, in every street of Paris preparations were going on for the enormous perpetration. Soldiers were assembling in different places of rendezvous. Guards were stationed at important points in the city, that their victims might not escape. Armed citizens, with loaded muskets and sabres gleaming in the lamplight, began to emerge, through the darkness, from their dwellings, and to gather, in motley and interminable assemblage, around the Hotel de Ville. A regiment of guards were stationed at the gates of the royal palace to protect Charles and Catharine from any possibility of danger. Many of the houses were illuminated, that by the light blazing from the windows, the bullet might be thrown with precision, and that the dagger might strike an unerring blow. Agitation and alarm pervaded the vast metropolis. The Catholics were rejoicing that the hour of vengeance had arrived. The Protestants gazed upon the portentous gatherings of this storm in utter bewilderment.

All the arrangements of the enterprise were left to the Duke of Guise, and a more efficient and fitting agent could not have been found. He had ordered that the tocsin, the signal for the massacre, should be tolled at two o'clock in the morning. Catharine and Charles, in one of the apartments of the palace of the Louvre, were impatiently awaiting the lingering flight of the hours till the alarm-bell should toll forth the death-warrant of their Protestant subjects. Catharine, inured to treachery and hardened in vice, was apparently a stranger to all compunctious visitings. A life of crime had steeled her soul against every merciful impression. But she was very apprehensive lest her son, less obdurate in purpose, might relent. Though impotent in character, he was, at times, petulant and self-willed, and in paroxysms of stubbornness spurned his mother's counsels and exerted his own despotic power.

Charles was now in a state of the most feverish excitement. He hastily paced the room, peering out at the window, and almost every moment looking at his watch, wishing that the hour would come, and again half regretting that the plot had been formed. The companions and the friends of his childhood, the invited guests who, for many weeks, had been his associates in gay festivities, and in the interchange of all kindly words and deeds, were, at his command, before the morning should dawn, to fall before the bullet and the poniard of the midnight murderer. His mother witnessed with intense anxiety this wavering of his mind. She therefore urged him no longer to delay, but to anticipate the hour, and to send a servant immediately to sound the alarm.

Charles hesitated, while a cold sweat ran from his forehead. "Are you a coward?" tauntingly inquired the fiendlike mother. This is the charge which will always make the poltroon squirm. The young king nervously exclaimed, "Well, then, begin."

There were in the chamber at the time only the king, his mother, and his brother the Duke of Anjou. A messenger was immediately dispatched to strike the bell. It was two hours after midnight. A few moments of terrible suspense ensued. There was a dead silence, neither of the three uttering a word. They all stood at the windows looking out into the rayless night. Suddenly, through the still air, the ponderous tones of the alarm-bell fell upon the ear, and rolled, the knell of death, over the city. Its vibrations awakened the demon in ten thousand hearts. It was the morning of the Sabbath, August 24th, 1572. It was the anniversary of a festival in honor of St. Bartholomew, which had long been celebrated. At the sound of the tocsin, the signal for the massacre, armed men rushed from every door into the streets, shouting, "*Vive Dieu et le roi!*"--*Live God and the king!*

CHAPTER V

MASSACRE OF ST. BARTHOLOMEW

1572

The commencement of the massacre.--The house forced.--Flight of the servants.--Death of Admiral Coligni.--Brutality.--Fate of the Duke of Guise.--Excitement of the Parisians.--Fiendish spirit of Charles.--Fugitives butchered.--Terror of Marguerite.--Flight of Marguerite.--Terrors of the night.--Remarkable escape of Maximilian.--Efforts to save his life.--The disguise.--Scene in the street.--The talisman.--Arrival at the college.--His protection.--Henry taken before the king.--He yields.--Paris on the Sabbath following.--Encouragement by the priests.--The massacre continued.--Exultation of the Catholics.--Triumphal procession.--Extent of the massacre.--Magnanimity of Catholic officers.--The Bishop of Lisieux.--Noble replies to the king's decree.--The higher law.--Attempted justification.--Punishment of Coligni.--Valor of the survivors.--Pledges of aid.--Prophecy of Knox.--Apology of the court.--Opinions of the courts of Europe.--Rejoicings at Rome.--Atrocity of the deed.--Results of the massacre.--Retribution.

As the solemn dirge from the steeple rang out upon the night air, the king stood at the window of the palace trembling in every nerve. Hardly had the first tones of the alarm-bell fallen upon his ear when the report of a musket was heard, and the first victim fell. The sound seemed to animate to frenzy the demoniac Catharine, while it almost froze the blood in the veins of the young monarch, and he passionately called out for the massacre to be stopped. It was too late. The train was fired, and could not be extinguished. The signal passed with the rapidity of sound from steeple to steeple, till not only Paris, but entire France, was roused. The roar of human passion, the crackling fire of musketry, and the shrieks of the wounded and the dying, rose and blended in one fearful din throughout the whole metropolis. Guns, pistols, daggers, were every where busy. Old men, terrified maidens, helpless infants, venerable matrons, were alike smitten, and mercy had no appeal which could touch the heart of the murderers.

The wounded Admiral Coligni was lying helpless upon his bed, surrounded by a few personal friends, as the uproar of the rising storm of human violence and rage rolled in upon their ears. The Duke of Guise, with three hundred soldiers, hastened to the lodgings of the admiral. The gates were immediately knocked down, and the sentinels stabbed. A servant, greatly terrified, rushed into the inner apartment where the wounded admiral was lying, and exclaimed,

"The house is forced, and there is no means of resisting."

"I have long since," said the admiral, calmly, "prepared myself to die. Save yourselves, my friends, if you can, for you can not defend my life. I commend my soul to the mercy of God."

The companions of the admiral, having no possible means of protection, and perhaps adding to his peril by their presence, immediately fled to other apartments of the house. They were pursued and stabbed. Three leaped from the windows and were shot in the streets.

Coligni, left alone in his apartment, rose with difficulty from his bed, and, being unable to stand, leaned for support against the wall. A desperado by the name of Breme, a follower of the Duke of Guise, with a congenial band of accomplices, rushed into the room. They saw a venerable man, pale, and with bandaged wounds, in his night-dress, engaged in prayer.

"Art thou the admiral?" demanded the assassin, with brandished sword.

"I am," replied the admiral; "and thou, young man, shouldst respect my gray hairs. Nevertheless, thou canst abridge my life but a little."

Breme plunged his sword into his bosom, and then withdrawing it, gave him a cut upon the head. The admiral fell, calmly saying, "If I could but die by the hand of a gentleman instead of such a knave as this!" The rest of the assassins then rushed upon him, piercing his body with their daggers.

The Duke of Guise, ashamed himself to meet the eye of this noble victim to the basest treachery, remained impatiently in the court-yard below.

"Breme!" he shouted, looking up at the window, "have you done it?"

"Yes," Breme exclaimed from the chamber, "he is done for."

"Let us see, though," rejoined the duke. "Throw the body from the window."

The mangled corpse was immediately thrown down upon the pavement of the court-yard. The duke, with his handkerchief, wiped the blood and the dirt from his face, and carefully scrutinized the features.

"Yes," said he, "I recognize him. He is the man."

Then giving the pallid cheek a kick, he exclaimed, "Courage, comrades! we have happily begun. Let us now go for others. The king commands it."

In sixteen years from this event the Duke of Guise was himself assassinated, and received a kick in the face from Henry III., brother of the same king in whose service he had drawn the dagger of the murderer. Thus died the Admiral Coligni, one of the noblest sons of France. Though but fifty-six years of age, he was prematurely infirm from care, and toil, and suffering.

For three days the body was exposed to the insults of the populace, and finally was hung up by the feet on a gibbet. A cousin of Coligni secretly caused it to be taken down and buried.

The tiger, having once lapped his tongue in blood, seems to be imbued with a new spirit of ferocity. There is in man a similar temper, which is roused and stimulated by carnage. The excitement of human slaughter converts man into a demon. The riotous multitude of Parisians was becoming each moment more and more clamorous for blood. They broke open the houses of the Protestants, and, rushing into their chambers, murdered indiscriminately both sexes and every age. The streets resounded with the shouts of the assassins and the shrieks of their victims. Cries of "Kill! kill! more blood!" rent the air. The bodies of the slain were thrown out of the windows into the streets, and the pavements of the city were clotted with human gore.

Charles, who was overwhelmed with such compunctions of conscience when he heard the first shot, and beheld from his window the commencement of the butchery, soon recovered from his momentary wavering, and, conscious that it was too late to draw back, with fiendlike eagerness engaged himself in the work of death. The monarch, when a boy, had been noted for his sanguinary spirit, delighting with his own hand to perform the revolting acts of the slaughter-house. Perfect fury seemed now to take possession of him. His cheeks were flushed, his lips compressed, his eyes glared with frenzy. Bending eagerly from his window, he shouted words of encouragement to the assassins. Grasping a gun, in the handling of which he had become very skillful from long practice in the chase, he watched, like a sportsman, for his prey; and when he saw an unfortunate Protestant, wounded and bleeding, flying from his pursuers, he would take deliberate aim from the window of his palace, and shout with exultation as he saw him fall, pierced by his bullet. A crowd of fugitives rushed into the court-yard of the Louvre to throw themselves upon the protection of the king. Charles sent his own body-guard into the yard, with guns and daggers, to butcher them all, and the pavements of the palace-yard were drenched with their blood.

[Illustration: THE MASSACRE OF ST. BARTHOLOMEW.]

Just before the carnage commenced, Marguerite, weary with excitement and the agitating conversation to which she had so long been listening, retired to her private apartment for sleep. She had hardly closed her eyes when the fearful outcries of the pursuers and the pursued filled the palace. She sprang up in her bed, and heard some one struggling at the door, and shrieking "Navarre! Navarre!" In a paroxysm of terror, she ordered an attendant to open the door. One of her husband's retinue instantly rushed in, covered with wounds and blood, pursued by four soldiers of her brother's guard. The captain of the guard entered at the same moment, and, at the earnest entreaty of the princess, spared her the anguish of seeing the friend of her husband murdered before her eyes.

Marguerite, half delirious with bewilderment and terror, fled from her room to seek the apartment of her sister. The palace was filled with uproar, the shouts of the assassins and the shrieks of their victims blending in awful confusion. As she was rushing through the hall, she encountered another Protestant gentleman flying before the dripping sword of his pursuer. He was covered with blood, flowing from the many wounds he had already received. Just as he reached the young Queen of Navarre, his pursuer overtook him and plunged a sword through his body. He fell dead at her feet.

No tongue can tell the horrors of that night. It would require volumes to record the frightful scenes which were enacted before the morning dawned. Among the most remarkable escapes we may mention that of a lad whose name afterward attained much celebrity. The Baron de Rosny, a Protestant lord of great influence and worth, had accompanied his son Maximilian, a very intelligent and spirited boy, about eleven years of age, to Paris, to attend the nuptials of the King of Navarre. This young prince, Maximilian, afterward the world-renowned Duke of Sully, had previously been prosecuting his studies in the College of Burgundy, in the metropolis, and had become a very great favorite of the warm-hearted King of Navarre. His father had come to Paris with great reluctance, for he had no confidence in the protestations of Catharine and Charles IX. Immediately after the attempt was made to assassinate the admiral, the Baron de Rosny, with many of his friends, left the city, intrusting his son to the care of a private tutor and a valet de chambre. He occupied lodgings in a remote quarter of the city and near the colleges.

Young Maximilian was asleep in his room, when, a little after midnight, he was aroused by the ringing of the alarm-bells, and the confused cries of the populace. His tutor and valet de chambre sprang from their beds, and hurried out to ascertain the cause of the tumult. They did not, however, return, for they had hardly reached the door when they were shot down. Maximilian, in great bewilderment respecting their continued absence, and the dreadful clamor continually increasing, was hurriedly dressing himself, when his landlord came in, pale and trembling, and informed him of the massacre which was going on, and that he had saved his own life only by the avowal of his faith in the Catholic religion. He earnestly urged Maximilian to do the same. The young prince magnanimously resolved not to save his life by falsehood and apostasy. He determined to attempt, in the darkness and confusion of the night, to gain the College of Burgundy, where he hoped to find some Catholic friends who would protect him.

The distance of the college from the house in which he was rendered the undertaking desperately perilous. Having disguised himself in the dress of a Roman Catholic priest, he took a large prayer-book under his arm, and tremblingly issued forth into the streets. The sights which met his eye in the gloom of that awful night were enough to appal the stoutest heart. The murderers, frantic with excitement and intoxication, were uttering wild outcries, and pursuing, in every direction, their terrified victims. Women and children, in their night-clothes, having just sprung in terror from their beds, were flying from their pursuers, covered with wounds, and uttering fearful shrieks. The mangled bodies of the young and of the old, of males and females, were strewn along the streets, and the pavements were slippery with blood. Loud and dreadful outcries were heard from the interior of the dwellings as the work of midnight assassination proceeded; and struggles of desperate violence were witnessed, as the murderers attempted to throw their bleeding and dying victims from the high windows of chambers and attics upon the pavements below. The shouts of the assailants, the shrieks of the wounded, as blow after blow fell upon them, the incessant reports of muskets and pistols, the tramp of soldiers, and the peals of the alarm-bell, all combined to create a scene of terror such as human eyes have seldom witnessed. In the midst of ten thousand perils, the young man crept along, protected by his priestly garb, while he frequently saw his fellow-Christians shot and stabbed at his very side.

Suddenly, in turning a corner, he fell into the midst of a band of the body-guard of the king, whose swords were dripping with blood. They seized him with great roughness, when, seeing the Catholic prayer-book which was in his hands, they considered it a safe passport, and permitted him to continue on his way uninjured. Twice again he encountered similar peril, as he was seized by bands of infuriated men, and each time he was extricated in the same way.

At length he arrived at the College of Burgundy; and now his danger increased tenfold. It was a Catholic college. The porter at the gate absolutely refused him admittance. The murderers began to multiply in the street around him with fierce and threatening questions. Maximilian at length, by inquiring for La Faye, the president of the college, and by placing a bribe in the hands of the porter, succeeded in obtaining entrance. La Faye was a humane man, and exceedingly attached to his Protestant pupil. Maximilian entered the apartment of the president, and found there two Catholic priests. The priests, as soon as they saw him, insisted upon cutting him down, declaring that the king had commanded that not even the infant at the breast should be spared. The good old man, however, firmly resolved to protect his young friend, and, conducting him privately to a secure chamber, locked him up. Here he remained three days in the greatest suspense, apprehensive every hour that the assassins would break in upon him. A faithful servant of the president brought him food, but could tell him of nothing but deeds of treachery and blood. At the end of three days, the heroic boy, who afterward attained great celebrity as the minister and bosom friend of Henry, was released and protected.

The morning of St. Bartholomew's day had not dawned when a band of soldiers entered the chamber of Henry of Navarre and conveyed him to the presence of the king. Frenzied with the excitements of the scene, the imbecile but passionate monarch received him with a countenance inflamed with fury. With blasphemous oaths and imprecations, he commanded the King of Navarre, as he valued his life, to abandon a religion which Charles affirmed that the Protestants had assumed only as a cloak for their rebellion. With violent gesticulations and threats, he declared that he would no longer submit to be contradicted by his subjects, but that they should revere him as the image of God. Henry, who was a Protestant from considerations of state policy rather than from Christian principle, and who saw in the conflict merely a strife between two political parties, ingloriously yielded to that necessity by which alone he could save his life. Charles gave him three days to deliberate, declaring, with a violent oath, that if, at the end of that time, he did not yield to his commands, he would cause him to be strangled. Henry yielded. He not only went to mass himself, but submitted to the degradation of sending an edict to his own dominions, prohibiting the exercise of any religion except that of Rome. This indecision was a serious blot upon his character. Energetic and decisive as he was in all his measures of government, his religious convictions were ever feeble and wavering.

When the darkness of night passed away and the morning of the Sabbath dawned upon Paris, a spectacle was witnessed such as the streets even of that blood-renowned metropolis have seldom presented. The city still resounded with that most awful of all tumults, the clamor of an infuriated mob. The pavements were covered with gory corpses. Men, women, and children were still flying in every direction, wounded and bleeding, pursued by merciless assassins, riotous with demoniac laughter and drunk with blood. The report of guns and pistols was heard in all parts of the city, sometimes in continuous volleys, as if platoons of soldiers were firing upon their victims, while the scattered shots, incessantly repeated in every section of the extended metropolis, proved the universality of the massacre. Drunken wretches, besmeared with blood, were swaggering along the streets, with ribald jests and demoniac howlings, hunting for the Protestants. Bodies, torn and gory, were hanging from the windows, and dissevered heads were spurned like footballs along the pavements. Priests were seen in their sacerdotal robes, with elevated crucifixes, and with fanatical exclamations encouraging the murderers not to grow weary in their holy work of exterminating God's enemies. The most distinguished nobles and generals of the court and the camp of Charles, mounted on horseback with gorgeous retinue, rode through the streets, encouraging by voice and arm the indiscriminate massacre.

"Let not," the king proclaimed, "one single Protestant be spared to reproach me hereafter with this deed."

For a whole week the massacre continued, and it was computed that from eighty to a hundred thousand Protestants were slain throughout the kingdom.

Charles himself, with Catharine and the highborn but profligate ladies who disgraced her court, emerged with the morning light, in splendid array, into the reeking streets. The ladies contemplated with merriment and ribald jests the dead bodies of the Protestants piled up before the Louvre. Some of the retinue, appalled by the horrid spectacle, wished to retire, alleging that the bodies already emitted a putrid odor. Charles inhumanly replied, "The smell of a dead

KARTINDO PUBLISHING HOUSE (Kartindo.Com)

enemy is always pleasant."

On Thursday, after four days spent in hunting out the fugitives and finishing the bloody work, the clergy paraded the streets in a triumphal procession, and with jubilant prayers and hymns gave thanks to God for their great victory. The Catholic pulpits resounded with exultant harangues, and in honor of the event a medallion was struck off, with the inscription "*La piété a reveille la justice*"-- *Religion has awakened justice.*

In the distant provinces of France the massacre was continued, as the Protestants were hunted from all their hiding-places. In some departments, as in Santonge and Lower Languedoc, the Protestants were so numerous that the Catholics did not venture to attack them. In some other provinces they were so few that the Catholics had nothing whatever to fear from them, and therefore spared them; and in the sparsely-settled rural districts the peasants refused to imbrue their hands in the blood of their neighbors. Many thousand Protestants throughout the kingdom in these ways escaped.

But in nearly all the populous towns, where the Catholic population predominated, the massacre was universal and indiscriminate. In Meaux, four hundred houses of Protestants were pillaged and devastated, and the inmates, without regard to age or sex, utterly exterminated. At Orleans there were three thousand Protestants. A troop of armed horsemen rode furiously through the streets, shouting, "Courage, boys! kill all, and then you shall divide their property." At Rouen, many of the Protestants, at the first alarm, fled. The rest were arrested and thrown into prison. They were then brought out one by one, and deliberately murdered. Six hundred were thus slain. Such were the scenes which were enacted in Toulouse, Bordeaux, Bourges, Angers, Lyons, and scores of other cities in France. It is impossible to ascertain with precision the number of victims. The Duke of Sully estimates them at seventy thousand; the Bishop Péréfixe at one hundred thousand. This latter estimate is probably not exaggerated, if we include the unhappy fugitives, who, fleeing from their homes, died of cold, hunger, and fatigue, and all the other nameless woes which accrued from this great calamity.

In the midst of these scenes of horror it is pleasant to record several instances of generous humanity. In the barbarism of those times dueling was a common practice. A Catholic officer by the name of Vessins, one of the most fierce and irritable men in France, had a private quarrel with a Protestant officer whose name was Regnier. They had mutually sought each other in Paris to obtain such satisfaction as a duel could afford. In the midst of the massacre, Regnier, while at prayers with his servant (for in those days dueling and praying were not deemed inconsistent), heard the door of his room broken open, and, looking round in expectation of instant death, saw his foe Vessins enter breathless with excitement and haste. Regnier, conscious that all resistance would be unavailing, calmly bared his bosom to his enemy, exclaiming,

"You will have an easy victory."

Vessins made no reply, but ordered the valet to seek his master's cloak and sword. Then leading him into the street, he mounted him upon a powerful horse, and with fifteen armed men escorted him out of the city. Not a word was exchanged between them. When they arrived at a little grove at a short distance from the residence of the Protestant gentleman, Vessins presented him with his sword, and bade him dismount and defend himself, saying,

"Do not imagine that I seek your friendship by what I have done. All I wish is to take your life honorably."

Regnier threw away his sword, saying, "I will never strike at one who has saved my life."

"Very well!" Vessins replied, and left him, making him a present of the horse on which he rode.

Though the commands which the king sent to the various provinces of France for the massacre were very generally obeyed, there were examples of distinguished virtue, in which Catholics of high rank not only refused to imbrue their own hands in blood, but periled their lives to protect the Protestants. The Bishop of Lisieux, in the exercise of true Christian charity, saved all the Protestants in the town over which he presided. The Governor of Auvergne replied to the secret letter of the king in the following words:

"Sire, I have received an order, under your majesty's seal, to put all the Protestants of this province to death, and if, which God forbid, the order be genuine, I respect your majesty still too much to obey you."

The king had sent a similar order to the commandant at Bayonne, the Viscount of Orthez. The following noble words were returned in reply:

"Sire, I have communicated the commands of your majesty to the inhabitants of the town and to the soldiers of the garrison, and I have found good citizens and brave soldiers, *but not one executioner*; on which account, they and I humbly beseech you to employ our arms and our lives in enterprises in which we can conscientiously engage. However perilous they may be, we will willingly shed therein the last drop of our blood."

Both of these noble-minded men soon after very suddenly and mysteriously died. Few entertained a doubt that poison had been administered by the order of Charles.

The *law* of France required that these Protestants should be hunted to death. This was *the law* promulgated by the king and sent by his own letters missive to the appointed officers of the crown.

But there is--*there is* a HIGHER LAW than that of kings and courts. Nobly these majestic men rendered to it their allegiance. They sealed their fidelity to this HIGHER LAW with their blood. They were martyrs, not fanatics.

On the third day of the massacre the king assembled the Parliament in Paris, and made a public avowal of the part he had taken in this fearful tragedy, and of the reasons which had influenced him to the deed. Though he hoped to silence all Protestant tongues in his own realms in death, he knew that the tale would be told throughout all Europe. He therefore stated, in justification of the act, that he had, "as if by a miracle," discovered that the Protestants were engaged in a conspiracy against his own life and that of all of his family.

This charge, however, uttered for the moment, was speedily dropped and forgotten. There was not the slightest evidence of such a design.

The Parliament, to give a little semblance of justice to the king's accusation, sat in judgment upon the memory of the noble Coligni. They sentenced him to be hung in effigy; ordered his arms to be dragged at the heels of a horse through all the principal towns of France; his magnificent castle of Chatillon to be razed to its foundations, and never to be rebuilt; his fertile acres, in the culture of which he had found his chief delight, to be desolated and sown with salt; his portraits and statues, wherever found, to be destroyed; his children to lose their title of nobility; all his goods and estates to be confiscated to the use of the crown, and a monument of durable marble to be raised, upon which this sentence of the court should be engraved, to transmit to all posterity his alleged

KARTINDO PUBLISHING HOUSE (Kartindo.Com)

infamy. Thus was punished on earth one of the noblest servants both of God and man. But there is a day of final judgment yet to come. The oppressor has but his brief hour. There is eternity to right the oppressed.

Notwithstanding this general and awful massacre, the Protestants were far from being exterminated. Several nobles, surrounded by their retainers in their distant castles, suspicious of treachery, had refused to go to Paris to attend the wedding of Henry and Marguerite. Others who had gone to Paris, alarmed by the attack upon Admiral Coligni, immediately retired to their homes. Some concealed themselves in garrets, cellars, and wells until the massacre was over. As has been stated, in some towns the governors refused to engage in the merciless butchery, and in others the Protestants had the majority, and with their own arms could defend themselves within the walls which their own troops garrisoned.

Though, in the first panic caused by the dreadful slaughter, the Protestants made no resistance, but either surrendered themselves submissively to the sword of the assassin, or sought safety in concealment or flight, soon indignation took the place of fear. Those who had fled from the kingdom to Protestant states rallied together. The survivors in France began to count their numbers and marshal their forces for self-preservation. From every part of Protestant Europe a cry of horror and execration simultaneously arose in view of this crime of unparalleled enormity. In many places the Catholics themselves seemed appalled in contemplation of the deed they had perpetrated. Words of sympathy were sent to these martyrs to a pure faith from many of the Protestant kingdoms, with pledges of determined and efficient aid. The Protestants rapidly gained courage. From all the country, they flocked into those walled towns which still remained in their power.

As the fugitives from France, emaciate, pale, and woe-stricken, with tattered and dusty garb, recited in England, Switzerland, and Germany the horrid story of the massacre, the hearts of their auditors were frozen with horror. In Geneva a day of fasting and prayer was instituted, which is observed even to the present day. In Scotland every church resounded with the thrilling tale; and Knox, whose inflexible spirit was nerved for those iron times, exclaimed, in language of prophetic nerve,

"Sentence has gone forth against that murderer, the King of France, and the vengeance of God will never be withdrawn from his house. His name shall be held in everlasting execration."

KARTINDO PUBLISHING HOUSE (Kartindo.Com)

The French court, alarmed by the indignation it had aroused, sent an embassador to London with a poor apology for the crime, by pretending that the Protestants had conspired against the life of the king. The embassador was received in the court of the queen with appalling coldness and gloom. Arrangements were made to invest the occasion with the most impressive solemnity. The court was shrouded in mourning, and all the lords and ladies appeared in sable weeds. A stern and sombre sadness was upon every countenance. The embassador, overwhelmed by his reception, was overheard to exclaim to himself, in bitterness of heart,

"I am ashamed to acknowledge myself a Frenchman."

He entered, however, the presence of the queen, passed through the long line of silent courtiers, who refused to salute him, or even to honor him with a look, stammered out his miserable apology, and, receiving no response, retired covered with confusion. Elizabeth, we thank thee! This one noble deed atones for many of thy crimes.

Very different was the reception of these tidings in the court of Rome. The messenger who carried the news was received with transports of joy, and was rewarded with a thousand pieces of gold. Cannons were fired, bells rung, and an immense procession, with all the trappings of sacerdotal rejoicing, paraded the streets. Anthems were chanted and thanksgivings were solemnly offered for the great victory over the enemies of the Church. A gold medal was struck off to commemorate the event; and Charles IX. and Catharine were pronounced, by the infallible word of his holiness, to be the especial favorites of God. Spain and the Netherlands united with Rome in these infamous exultations. Philip II. wrote from Madrid to Catharine,

"These tidings are the greatest and the most glorious I could have received."

Such was the awful massacre of St. Bartholomew. When contemplated in all its aspects of perfidy, cruelty, and cowardice, it must be pronounced the greatest crime recorded in history. The victims were invited under the guise of friendship to Paris. They were received with solemn oaths of peace and protection. The leading men in the nation placed the dagger in the hands of an ignorant and degraded people. The priests, professed ministers of Jesus Christ, stimulated the benighted multitude by all the appeals of fanaticism to exterminate those whom they denounced as the enemies of God and man. After the great atrocity was perpetrated, princes and priests, with blood-stained

KARTINDO PUBLISHING HOUSE (Kartindo.Com)

hands, flocked to the altars of God, our common Father, to thank him that the massacre had been accomplished.

The annals of the world are filled with narratives of crime and woe, but the Massacre of St. Bartholomew stands perhaps without a parallel.

It has been said, "The blood of the martyrs is the seed of the Church." This is only true with exceptions. Protestantism in France has never recovered from this blow. But for this massacre one half of the nobles of France would have continued Protestant. The Reformers would have constituted so large a portion of the population that mutual toleration would have been necessary. Henry IV. would not have abjured the Protestant faith. Intelligence would have been diffused; religion would have been respected; and in all probability, the horrors of the French Revolution would have been averted.

God is an avenger. In the mysterious government which he wields, mysterious only to our feeble vision, he "visits the iniquities of the fathers upon the children, even unto the third and fourth generation." As we see the priests of Paris and of France, during the awful tragedy of the Revolution, massacred in the prisons, shot in the streets, hung upon the lamp-posts, and driven in starvation and woe from the kingdom, we can not but remember the day of St. Bartholomew. The 24th of August, 1572, and the 2d of September, 1792, though far apart in the records of time, are consecutive days in the government of God.

KARTINDO PUBLISHING HOUSE (Kartindo.Com)

CHAPTER VI

THE HOUSES OF VALOIS, OF GUISE, AND OF BOURBON

Illustrious French families.--The house of Valois.--Early condition of France.--Clovis.--The Carlovingian dynasty.--Capet and Philip.--Decay of the house of Valois.--House of Guise.--The dukedom of Lorraine.--Claude of Lorraine.--Marriage of the Count of Guise.--Francis I.--The suggestion and its results.--Bravery of the duke.--His prominence.--Days of war.--The bloody rout.--Scene from the castle.--Claude the Butcher.--The Cardinal of Lorraine.--The reprimand.--Duke of Mayence.--The family of Guise.--Henry the Eighth.--Death of Claude.--Francis, Duke of Guise.--The dreadful wound.--Le Balafré.--Interview with the king.--Jealousy of the king.--Arrogance of the Guises.--Power of the house of Guise.--Appointment of Francis.--Thralldom of Henry II.--Mary, Queen of Scots.--Francis II.--Troubles between the Protestants and Catholics.--Admiral Coligni.--Antoinette.--Massacre by the Duke of Guise.--The Butcher of Vassy.--Remonstrance to the queen.--Magnanimity of the Duke of Guise.--Religious wars.--Assassination of the Duke of Guise.--Death of the duke.--Jean Poltrot.--Anecdote.--Prediction of Francis.--Enthusiasm of the populace.--The house of Bourbon.--The houses united.

At this time, in France, there were three illustrious and rival families, prominent above all others. Their origin was lost in the remoteness of antiquity. Their renown had been accumulating for many generations, through rank, and wealth, and power, and deeds of heroic and semi-barbarian daring. As these three families are so blended in all the struggles of this most warlike period, it is important to give a brief history of their origin and condition.

1. *The House of Valois.* More than a thousand years before the birth of Christ, we get dim glimpses of France, or, as it was then called, Gaul. It was peopled by a barbarian race, divided into petty tribes or clans, each with its chieftain, and each possessing undefined and sometimes almost unlimited power. Age after age rolled on, during which generations came and went like ocean billows, and all Gaul was but a continued battle-field. The history of each individual of its countless millions seems to have been, that he was born, killed as many of his fellow-creatures as he could, and then, having acquired thus much of glory, died.

About fifty years before the birth of Christ, Cæsar, with his conquering hosts, swept through the whole country, causing its rivers to run red with blood, until the subjugated Gauls submitted to Roman sway. In the decay of the Roman empire, about four hundred years after Christ, the Franks, from Germany, a barbarian horde as ferocious as wolves, penetrated the northern portion of Gaul, and, obtaining permanent settlement there, gave the whole country the name of France. Clovis was the chieftain of this warlike tribe. In the course of a few years, France was threatened with another invasion by combined hordes of barbarians from the north. The chiefs of the several independent tribes in France found it necessary to unite to repel the foe. They chose Clovis as their leader. This was the origin of the French monarchy. He was but little elevated above the surrounding chieftains, but by intrigue and power perpetuated his supremacy. For about three hundred years the family of Clovis retained its precarious and oft-contested elevation. At last, this line, enervated by luxury, became extinct, and another family obtained the throne. This new dynasty, under Pepin, was called the Carlovingian. The crown descended generally from father to son for about two hundred years, when the last of the race was poisoned by his wife. This family has been rendered very illustrious, both by Pepin and by his son, the still more widely renowned Charlemagne.

Hugh Capet then succeeded in grasping the sceptre, and for three hundred years the Capets held at bay the powerful chieftains who alternately assailed and defended the throne. Thirteen hundred years after Christ, the last of the Capets was borne to his tomb, and the feudal lords gave the pre-eminence to Philip of Valois. For about two hundred years the house of Valois had reigned. At the period of which we treat in this history, luxury and vice had brought the family near to extinction.

Charles IX., who now occupied the throne under the rigorous rule of his infamous mother, was feeble in body and still more feeble in mind. He had no child, and there was no probability that he would ever be blessed with an heir. His exhausted constitution indicated that a premature death was his inevitable destiny. His brother Henry, who had been elected King of Poland, would then succeed to the throne; but he had still less of manly character than Charles. An early death was his unquestioned doom. At his death, if childless, the house of Valois would become extinct. Who then should grasp the rich prize of the sceptre of France? The house of Guise and the house of Bourbon were rivals for this honor, and were mustering their strength and arraying their forces for the anticipated conflict. Each family could bring such vast influences into the struggle that no one could imagine in whose favor victory would decide. Such was the condition of the house of Valois in France in the year 1592.

KARTINDO PUBLISHING HOUSE (Kartindo.Com)

2. Let us now turn to the house of Guise. No tale of fiction can present a more fascinating collection of romantic enterprises and of wild adventures than must be recorded by the truthful historian of the house of Guise. On the western banks of the Rhine, between that river and the Meuse, there was the dukedom of Lorraine. It was a state of no inconsiderable wealth and power, extending over a territory of about ten thousand square miles, and containing a million and a half of inhabitants. Rene II., Duke of Lorraine, was a man of great renown, and in all the pride and pomp of feudal power he energetically governed his little realm. His body was scarred with the wounds he had received in innumerable battles, and he was ever ready to head his army of fifty thousand men, to punish any of the feudal lords around him who trespassed upon his rights.

The wealthy old duke owned large possessions in Normandy, Picardy, and various other of the French provinces. He had a large family. His fifth son, Claude, was a proud-spirited boy of sixteen. Rene sent this lad to France, and endowed him with all the fertile acres, and the castles, and the feudal rights which, in France, pertained to the noble house of Lorraine. Young Claude of Lorraine was presented at the court of St. Cloud as the Count of Guise, a title derived from one of his domains. His illustrious rank, his manly beauty, his princely bearing, his energetic mind, and brilliant talents, immediately gave him great prominence among the glittering throng of courtiers. Louis XII. was much delighted with the young count, and wished to attach the powerful and attractive stranger to his own house by an alliance with his daughter. The heart of the proud boy was, however, captivated by another beauty who embellished the court of the monarch, and, turning from the princess royal, he sought the hand of Antoinette, an exceedingly beautiful maiden of about his own age, a daughter of the house of Bourbon. The wedding of this young pair was celebrated with great magnificence in Paris, in the presence of the whole French court. Claude was then but sixteen years of age.

A few days after this event the infirm old king espoused the young and beautiful sister of Henry VIII. of England. The Count of Guise was honored with the commission of proceeding to Boulogne with several princes of the blood to receive the royal bride. Louis soon died, and his son, Francis I., ascended the throne. Claude was, by marriage, his cousin. He could bring all the influence of the proud house of Bourbon and the powerful house of Lorraine in support of the king. His own energetic, fearless, war-loving spirit invested him with great power in those barbarous days of violence and blood. Francis received his young cousin into high favor. Claude was, indeed, a young man of very rare accomplishments. His prowess in the jousts and tournaments, then so common, and his grace and magnificence in the drawing-room, rendered him an object of universal admiration.

One night Claude accompanied Francis I. to the queen's circle. She had gathered around her the most brilliant beauty of her realm. In those days woman occupied a very inferior position in society, and seldom made her appearance in the general assemblages of men. The gallant young count was fascinated with the amiability and charms of those distinguished ladies, and suggested to the king the expediency of breaking over the restraints which long usage had imposed, and embellishing his court with the attractions of female society and conversation. The king immediately adopted the welcome suggestion, and decided that, throughout the whole realm, women should be freed from the unjust restraint to which they had so long been subject. Guise had already gained the good-will of the nobility and of the army, and he now became a universal favorite with the ladies, and was thus the most popular man in France. Francis I. was at this time making preparations for the invasion of Italy, and the Count of Guise, though but eighteen years of age, was appointed commander-in-chief of a division of the army consisting of twenty thousand men.

In all the perils of the bloody battles which soon ensued, he displayed that utter recklessness of danger which had been the distinguishing trait of his ancestors. In the first battle, when discomfiture and flight were spreading through his ranks, the proud count refused to retire one step before his foes. He was surrounded, overmatched, his horse killed from under him, and he fell, covered with twenty-two wounds, in the midst of the piles of mangled bodies which strewed the ground. He was afterward dragged from among the dead, insensible and apparently lifeless, and conveyed to his tent, where his vigorous constitution, and that energetic vitality which seemed to characterize his race, triumphed over wounds whose severity rendered their cure almost miraculous.

Francis I., in his report of the battle, extolled in the most glowing terms the prodigies of valor which Guise had displayed. War, desolating war, still ravaged wretched Europe, and Guise, with his untiring energy, became so prominent in the court and the camp that he was regarded rather as an ally of the King of France than as his subject. His enormous fortune, his ancestral renown, the vast political and military influences which were at his command, made him almost equal to the monarch whom he served. Francis lavished honors upon him, converted one of his counties into a dukedom, and, as *duke* of Guise, young Claude of Lorraine had now attained the highest position which a subject could occupy.

Years of conflagration, carnage, and woe rolled over war-deluged Europe, during which all the energies of the human race seemed to be expended in destruction; and in almost every scene of smouldering cities, of ravaged valleys, of battle-fields rendered hideous with the shouts of onset and shrieks of despair, we see the apparition of the stalwart frame of Guise, scarred, and war-worn, and blackened with the smoke and dust of the fray, riding upon his proud charger, wherever peril was most imminent, as if his body were made of iron.

At one time he drove before him, in most bloody rout, a numerous army of Germans. The fugitives, spreading over leagues of country, fled by his own strong castle of Neufchâteau. Antoinette and the ladies of her court stood upon the battlements of the castle, gazing upon the scene, to them so new and to them so pleasantly exciting. As they saw the charges of the cavalry trampling the dead and the dying beneath their feet, as they witnessed all the horrors of that most horrible scene which earth can present--a victorious army cutting to pieces its flying foes, with shouts of applause they animated the ardor of the victors. The once fair-faced boy had now become a veteran. His bronzed cheek and sinewy frame attested his life of hardship and toil. The nobles were jealous of his power. The king was annoyed by his haughty bearing; but he was the idol of the people. In one campaign he caused the death of forty thousand Protestants, for he was the devoted servant of mother Church. *Claude the Butcher* was the not inappropriate name by which the Protestants designated him. His brother John attained the dignity of Cardinal of Lorraine. Claude with his keen sword, and John with pomp, and pride, and spiritual power, became the most relentless foes of the Reformation, and the most valiant defenders of the Catholic faith.

The kind-heartedness of the wealthy but dissolute cardinal, and the prodigality of his charity, rendered him almost as popular as his warlike brother. When he went abroad, his *valet de chambre* invariably prepared him a bag filled with gold, from which he gave to the poor most freely. His reputation for charity was so exalted that a poor blind mendicant, to whom he gave gold in the streets of Rome, overjoyed at the acquisition of such a treasure, exclaimed, "Surely thou art either Christ or the Cardinal of Lorraine."

The Duke of Guise, in his advancing years, was accompanied to the field of battle by his son Francis, who inherited all of his father's courtly bearing, energy, talent, and headlong valor. At the siege of Luxemburg a musket ball shattered the ankle of young Francis, then Count of Aumale, and about eighteen years of age. As the surgeon was operating upon the splintered bones and quivering nerves, the sufferer gave some slight indication of his sense of pain.

KARTINDO PUBLISHING HOUSE (Kartindo.Com)

His iron father severely reprimanded him, saying,

"Persons of your rank should not feel their wounds, but, on the contrary, should take pleasure in building up their reputation upon the ruin of their bodies."

Others of the sons of Claude also signalized themselves in the wars which then desolated Europe, and they received wealth and honors. The king erected certain lands and lordships belonging to the Duke of Guise into a marquisate, and then immediately elevated the marquisate into a duchy, and the youngest son of the Duke of Guise, inheriting the property, was ennobled with the title of the Duke of Mayence. Thus there were two rich dukedoms in the same family.

Claude had six sons, all young men of imperious spirit and magnificent bearing. They were allied by marriage with the most illustrious families in France, several of them being connected with princes of the blood royal. The war-worn duke, covered with wounds which he deemed his most glorious ornaments, often appeared at court accompanied by his sons. They occupied the following posts of rank and power: Francis, the eldest, Count of Aumale, was the heir of the titles and the estates of the noble house. Claude was Marquis of Mayence; Charles was Archbishop of Rheims, the richest benefice in France, and he soon attained one of the highest dignities of the Church by the reception of a cardinal's hat; Louis was Bishop of Troyes, and Francis, the youngest, Chevalier of Lorraine and Duke of Mayence, was general of the galleys of France. One of the daughters was married to the King of Scotland, and the others had formed most illustrious connections. Thus the house of Guise towered proudly and sublimely from among the noble families in the midst of whom it had so recently been implanted.

Henry VIII. of England, inflamed by the report of the exceeding beauty of Mary, daughter of the Duke of Guise, had solicited her hand; but Claude was unwilling to surrender his daughter to England's burly and brutal old tyrant, and declined the regal alliance. The exasperated monarch, in revenge, declared war against France. Years of violence and blood lingered away. At last Claude, aged and infirm, surrendered to that king of terrors before whom all must bow. In his strong castle of Joinville, on the twelfth of April, 1550, the illustrious, magnanimous, blood-stained duke, after a whole lifetime spent in slaughter, breathed his last. His children and his grandchildren were gathered around the bed of the dying chieftain. In the darkness of that age, he felt that he had been contending, with divine approval, for Christ and his Church. With prayers and thanksgivings, and language expressive of meekness and humility before God, he ascended to that tribunal of final judgment where there is no difference between the peasant and the prince.

The chivalrous and warlike Francis inherited his father's titles, wealth, and power; and now the house of Guise was so influential that the king trembled in view of its rivalry. It was but the kingly office alone which rendered the house of Valois superior to the house of Guise. In illustration of the character of those times, and the hardihood and sufferings through which the renown of these chieftains was obtained, the following anecdote may be narrated.

Francis, Duke of Guise, in one of the skirmishes with the English invaders, received a wound which is described as the most severe from which any one ever recovered. The lance of an English officer "entered above the right eye, declining toward the nose, and piercing through on the other side, between the nape and the ear." The weapon, having thus penetrated the head more than half a foot, was broken off by the violence of the blow, the lance-iron and two fingers' breadth of the staff remaining in the dreadful wound. The surgeons of the army, stupefied by the magnitude of the injury, declined to attempt the extraction of the splinter, saying that it would only expose him to dreadful and unavailing suffering, as he must inevitably die. The king immediately sent his surgeon, with orders to spare no possible efforts to save the life of the hero. The lance-head was broken off so short that it was impossible to grasp it with the hand. The surgeon took the heavy pincers of a blacksmith, and asked the sufferer if he would allow him to make use of so rude an instrument, and would also permit him to place his foot upon his face.

"You may do any thing you consider necessary," said the duke.

The officers standing around looked on with horror as the king's surgeon, aided by an experienced practitioner, tore out thus violently the barbed iron, fracturing the bones, and tearing nerves, veins, and arteries. The hardy soldier bore the anguish without the contraction of a muscle, and was only heard gently to exclaim to himself, "Oh my God!" The sufferer recovered, and ever after regarded the frightful scar which was left as a signal badge of honor. He hence bore the common name of Le Balafré, or *The Scarred*.

As the duke returned to court, the king hurried forth from his chamber to meet him, embraced him warmly, and said,

"It is fair that I should come out to meet my old friend, who, on his part, is ever so ready to meet my enemies."

KARTINDO PUBLISHING HOUSE (Kartindo.Com)

Gradually, however, Francis, the king, became very jealous of the boundless popularity and enormous power acquired by this ambitious house. Upon his dying bed he warned his son of the dangerous rivalry to which the Guises had attained, and enjoined it upon him to curb their ambition by admitting none of the princes of that house to a share in the government; but as soon as King Francis was consigned to his tomb, Henry II., his son and successor, rallied the members of this family around him, and made the duke almost the partner of his throne. He needed the support of the strong arm and of the inexhaustible purse of the princes of Lorraine.

The arrogance of the Guises, or the princes of Lorraine, as they were frequently called, in consequence of their descent from Claude of Lorraine, reached such a pitch that on the occasion of a proud pageant, when Henry II. was on a visit of inspection to one of his frontier fortresses, the Duke of Guise claimed equal rank with Henry of Navarre, who was not only King of Navarre, but, as the Duke of Vendôme, was also first prince of the blood in France. An angry dispute immediately arose. The king settled it in favor of the audacious Guise, for he was intimidated by the power of that arrogant house. He thus exasperated Henry of Navarre, and also nurtured the pride of a dangerous rival.

All classes were now courting the Duke of Guise. The first nobles of the land sought his protection and support by flattering letters and costly presents. "From all quarters," says an ancient manuscript, "he received offerings of wine, fruit, confections, ortolans, horses, dogs, hawks, and gerfalcons. The letters accompanying these often contained a second paragraph petitioning for pensions or grants from the king, or for places, even down to that of apothecary or of barber to the Dauphin." The monarchs of foreign countries often wrote to him soliciting his aid. The duke, in the enjoyment of this immense wealth, influence, and power, assumed the splendors of royalty, and his court was hardly inferior to that of the monarch. The King of Poland and the Duke of Guise were rivals for the hand of Anne, the beautiful daughter of the Duke of Ferrara, and Guise was the successful suitor.

Francis of Lorraine was now appointed lieutenant general of the French armies, and the king addressed to all the provincial authorities special injunction to render as prompt and absolute obedience to the orders of the Duke of Guise as if they emanated from himself. "And truly," says one of the writers of those times, "never had monarch in France been obeyed more punctually or with greater zeal." In fact, Guise was now the head of the government, and all the great interests of the nation were ordered by his mind. Henry was a feeble prince, with neither vigor of body nor energy of intellect to resist the encroachments of so imperial a spirit. He gave many indications of uneasiness in view of his own thralldom, but he was entirely unable to dispense with the aid of his sagacious ally.

It will be remembered that one of the daughters of Claude, and a sister of Francis, the second duke of Guise, married the King of Scotland. Her daughter, the niece of Francis, was the celebrated Mary, Queen of Scots. She had been sent to France for her education, and she was married, when very young, to her cousin Francis, son of Henry II. and of the infamous Catharine de Medici. He was heir of the French throne. This wedding was celebrated with the utmost magnificence, and the Guises moved on the occasion through the palaces of royalty with the pride of monarchs. Henry II. was accidentally killed in a tournament; and Francis, his son, under the title of Francis II., with his young and beautiful bride, the unfortunate Mary, Queen of Scots, ascended the throne. Francis was a feeble-minded, consumptive youth of 16, whose thoughts were all centred in his lovely wife. Mary, who was but fifteen years of age, was fascinating in the extreme, and entirely devoted to pleasure. She gladly transferred all the power of the realm to her uncles, the Guises.

About this time the conflict between the Catholics and the Protestants began to grow more violent. The Catholics drew the sword for the extirpation of heresy; the Protestants grasped their arms to defend themselves. The Guises consecrated all their energies to the support of the Papal Church and to the suppression of the Reformation. The feeble boy, Francis II., sat languidly upon his throne but seventeen months, when he died, on the 5th of December, 1560, and his brother, Charles IX., equally enervated in mind and with far less moral worth, succeeded to the crown. The death of Francis II. was a heavy blow to the Guises. The Admiral Coligni, one of the most illustrious of the Protestants, and the bosom friend of Henry of Navarre, was standing, with many other nobles, at the bedside of the monarch as he breathed his last.

"Gentlemen," said the admiral, with that gravity which was in accordance with his character and his religious principles, "the king is dead. It is a lesson to teach us all how to live."

The Protestants could not but rejoice that the Guises had thus lost the peculiar influence which they had secured from their near relationship to the queen. Admiral Coligni retired from the death-bed of the monarch to his own mansion, and, sitting down by the fire, became lost in the most profound reverie. He did not observe that his boots were burning until one of his friends called his attention to the fact.

"Ah!" he replied, "not a week ago, you and I would each have given a leg to have things take this turn, and now we get off with a pair of boots."

Antoinette, the widow of Claude of Lorraine, and the mother of Francis, the then Duke of Guise, was still living. She was so rancorous in her hostility to the Protestants that she was designated by them "*Mother of the tyrants and enemies of the Gospel*." Greatly to her annoyance, a large number of Protestants conducted their worship in the little town of Vassy, just on the frontier of the domains of the Duke of Guise. She was incessantly imploring her son to drive off these obnoxious neighbors. The duke was at one time journeying with his wife. Their route lay through the town of Vassy. His suite consisted of two hundred and sixty men at arms, all showing the warlike temper of their chief, and even far surpassing him in bigoted hatred of the Protestants.

On arriving at Vassy, the duke entered the church to hear high mass. It is said that while engaged in this act of devotion his ears were annoyed by the psalms of the Protestants, who were assembled in the vicinity. He sent an imperious message for the minister and the leading members of the congregation immediately to appear before him. The young men fulfilled their mission in a manner so taunting and insulting that a quarrel ensued, shots were exchanged, and immediately all the vassals of the duke, who were ripe for a fray, commenced an indiscriminate massacre. The Protestants valiantly but unavailingly defended themselves with sticks and stones; but the bullets of their enemies reached them everywhere, in the houses, on the roofs, in the streets. For an hour the carnage continued unchecked, and sixty men and women were killed and two hundred wounded. One only of the men of the duke was killed. Francis was ashamed of this slaughter of the defenseless, and declared that it was a sudden outbreak, for which he was not responsible, and which he had done every thing in his power to check; but ever after this he was called by the Protestants "*The Butcher of Vassy*."

When the news of this massacre reached Paris, Theodore de Beza was deputed by the Protestants to demand of Catharine, their regent, severe justice on the Duke of Guise; but Catharine feared the princes of Lorraine, and said to Beza,

"Whoever touches so much as the finger-tip of the Duke of Guise, touches me in the middle of my heart."

Beza meekly but courageously replied, "It assuredly behooves that Church of God, in whose name I speak, to endure blows and not to strike them; but may it please your majesty also to remember that it is an anvil which has worn out many hammers."

At the siege of Rouen the Duke of Guise was informed that an assassin had been arrested who had entered the camp with the intention of taking his life. He ordered the man to be brought before him, and calmly inquired,

"Have you not come hither to kill me?"

The intrepid but misguided young man openly avowed his intention.

"And what motive," inquired the duke, "impelled you to such a deed? Have I done you any wrong?"

"No," he replied; "but in removing you from the world I should promote the best interests of the Protestant religion, which I profess."

"My religion, then," generously replied the duke, "is better than yours, for it commands me to pardon, of my own accord, you who are convicted of guilt." And, by his orders, the assassin was safely conducted out of camp.

"A fine example," exclaims his historian, "of truly religious sentiments and magnanimous proselytism very natural to the Duke of Guise, the most moderate and humane of the chiefs of the Catholic army, and whose brilliant generosity had been but temporarily obscured by the occurrence at Vassy."

The war between the Catholics and Protestants was now raging with implacable fury, and Guise, victorious in many battles, had acquired from the Catholic party the name of "Savior of his Country." The duke was now upon the very loftiest summits of power which a subject can attain. In great exaltation of spirits, he one morning left the army over which he was commander-in-chief to visit the duchess, who had come to meet him at the neighboring castle of Corney. The duke very imprudently took with him merely one general officer and a page. It was a beautiful morning in February. As he crossed, in a boat, the mirrored surface of the Loiret, the vegetation of returning spring and the songs of the rejoicing birds strikingly contrasted with the blood, desolation, and misery with which the hateful spirit of war was desolating France. The duke was silent, apparently lost in painful reveries. His companions disturbed not his thoughts. Having crossed the stream, he was slowly walking his horse, with the reins hanging listlessly upon his mane, when a pistol was discharged at him from behind a hedge, at a distance of but six or seven paces. Two bullets pierced his side. On feeling himself wounded, he calmly said,

"They have long had this shot in reserve for me. I deserve it for my want of precaution."

[Illustration: THE ASSASSINATION OF FRANCIS, DUKE OF GUISE.]

He immediately fell upon his horse's neck, and was caught in the arms of his friends. They conveyed him to the castle, where the duchess received him with cries of anguish. He embraced her tenderly, minutely described the circumstances of his assassination, and expressed himself grieved in view of the stain which such a crime would inflict upon the honor of France. He exhorted his wife to bow in submission to the will of Heaven, and kissing his son Henry, the Duke of Joinville, who was weeping by his side, gently said to him,

"God grant thee grace, my son, to be a good man."

Thus died Francis, the second Duke of Guise, on the twenty-fourth of February, 1563. His murderer was a young Protestant noble, Jean Poltrot, twenty-four years of age. Poltrot, from being an ardent Catholic, had embraced the Protestant faith. This exposed him to persecution, and he was driven from France with the loss of his estates. He was compelled to support himself by manual labor. Soured in disposition, exasperated and half maddened, he insanely felt that he would be doing God service by the assassination of the *Butcher of Vassy*, the most formidable foe of the Protestant religion. It was a day of general darkness, and of the confusion of all correct ideas of morals.

Henry, the eldest son of the Duke of Guise, a lad of but thirteen years of age, now inherited the titles and the renown which his bold ancestors had accumulated. This was the Duke of Guise who was the bandit chieftain in the Massacre of St. Bartholomew.

One day Henry II. was holding his little daughter Marguerite, who afterward became the wife of Henry of Navarre, in his lap, when Henry of Guise, then Prince of Joinville, and the Marquis of Beaupreau, were playing together upon the floor, the one being but seven years of age, and the other but nine.

"Which of the two do you like the best?" inquired the king of his child.

"I prefer the marquis," she promptly replied.

"Yes; but the Prince of Joinville is the handsomest," the king rejoined.

"Oh," retorted Marguerite, "he is always in mischief, and he will be master every where."

Francis, the Duke of Guise, had fully apprehended the ambitious, impetuous, and reckless character of his son. He is said to have predicted that Henry, intoxicated by popularity, would perish in the attempt to seat himself upon the throne of France.

"Henry," says a writer of those times, "surpassed all the princes of his house in certain natural gifts, in certain talents, which procured him the respect of the court, the affection of the people, but which, nevertheless, were tarnished by a singular alloy of great faults and unlimited ambition."

"France was mad about that man," writes another, "for it is too little to say that she was in love with him. Her passion approached idolatry. There were persons who invoked him in their prayers. His portrait was every where. Some ran after him in the streets to touch his mantle with their rosaries. One day that he entered Paris on his return from a journey, the multitude not only cried '*Vive Guise!*' but many sang, on his passage, '*Hosanna to the son of David!*'"

3. *The House of Bourbon.* The origin of this family fades away in the remoteness of antiquity. Some bold chieftain, far remote in barbarian ages, emerged from obscurity and laid the foundations of the illustrious house. Generation after generation passed away, as the son succeeded the father in baronial pomp, and pride, and power, till the light of history, with its steadily-increasing brilliancy, illumined Europe. The family had often been connected in marriage both with the house of Guise and the royal line, the house of Valois. Antony of Bourbon, a sturdy soldier, united the houses of Bourbon and Navarre by marrying Jeanne d'Albret, the only child of the King of Navarre. Henry came from the union, an only son; and he, by marrying Marguerite, the daughter of the King of France, united the houses of Bourbon, Navarre, and Valois, and became heir to the throne of France should the sons of Henry II. die without issue.

This episode in reference to the condition of France at the time of which we write seems necessary to enable the reader fully to understand the succeeding chapters.

KARTINDO PUBLISHING HOUSE (Kartindo.Com)

CHAPTER VII

THE DEATH OF CHARLES IX AND THE ACCESSION OF HENRY III

1576-1577

Henry, King of Poland.--Henry's journey through Germany.--Enmity between the two brothers.--Sickness of Charles IX.--Remorse of the king.--Death of Charles IX.--Chateaubriand.--Character of the king.--Henry III.--The stratagem.--Flight from the crown.--The sojourn in Italy.--The three Henrys.--Marriage of Henry III.--The Duke of Alençon.--Suspicions of poison.--Invectives of the king.--Recovery of the king.--Disappointment of Francis.--Fanaticism of the king.--Escape of the Duke of Alençon.--The king aroused.--War of the public good.--Defeat of Guise.--Perplexity of Catharine.--The guard of honor.--Plan of escape.--Successful artifice.--The false rumor.--Escape accomplished.--Trouble of the Duke of Alençon.--Terms of settlement.--Paix de Monsieur.--Duke of Anjou.--Arrival at Rochelle.--Conduct of Catharine and Henry III.--Complexity of politics.--Francis and Queen Elizabeth.--New assaults on the Protestants.--Anecdote of the Protestants.--Gratitude of the citizens of Bayonne.--Anecdote of Henry of Navarre.--Another peace.--The battle arrested.--Pledge of peace.--Morality in France.--Disgraceful fête.--Murder in the royal palace.

After the Massacre of St. Bartholomew, a large number of the Protestants threw themselves into the city of Rochelle. For seven months they were besieged by all the power which the King of France could bring against them. They were at length, weakened by sickness and exhausted by famine, compelled to surrender. By their valiant resistance, however, they obtained highly honorable terms, securing for the inhabitants of Rochelle the free exercise of their religion within the walls of the city, and a general act of amnesty for all the Protestants in the realm.

Immediately after this event, Henry, the brother of Charles IX., was elected King of Poland, an honor which he attained in consequence of the military prowess he had displayed in the wars against the Protestants of France. Accompanied by his mother, Catharine de Medici, the young monarch set out for his distant dominions. Henry had been a very active agent in the Massacre of St. Bartholomew. At Lorraine Catharine took leave of him, and he went on his way in a very melancholy mood. His election had been secured by the greatest efforts of intrigue and bribery on the part of his mother. The melancholy countenances of the Protestants, driven into exile, and bewailing the murder of friends and relatives, whose assassination he had caused, met him at every turn. His reception at the German courts was cold and repulsive. In the palace of the Elector Palatine, Henry beheld the portrait of Coligni, who had been so treacherously slaughtered in the Massacre of St. Bartholomew. The portrait was suspended in a very conspicuous place of honor, and beneath it were inscribed the words,

"SUCH WAS THE FORMER COUNTENANCE OF THE HERO COLIGNI, WHO HAS BEEN RENDERED TRULY ILLUSTRIOUS BOTH BY HIS LIFE AND HIS DEATH."

The Protestant Elector pointed out the picture to the young king, whom he both hated and despised, and coolly asked him if he knew the man. Henry, not a little embarrassed, replied that he did.

"He was," rejoined the German prince, "the most honest man, and the wisest and the greatest captain of Europe, whose children I keep with me, lest the dogs of France should tear them as their father has been torn."

Thus Henry, gloomy through the repulses which he was ever encountering, journeyed along to Poland, where he was crowned king, notwithstanding energetic remonstrances on the part of those who execrated him for his deeds. The two brothers, Charles IX. and Henry, were bitter enemies, and Charles had declared, with many oaths, that one of the two should leave the realm. Henry was the favorite of Catharine, and hence she made such efforts to secure his safety by placing him upon the throne of Poland. She was aware that the feeble Charles would not live long, and when, with tears, she took leave of Henry, she assured him that he would soon return.

The outcry of indignation which the Massacre of St. Bartholomew called forth from combined Europe fell like the knell of death on the ear of the depraved and cowardly Charles. Disease began to ravage, with new violence, his exhausted frame. He became silent, morose, irritable, and gloomy. He secluded himself from all society, and surrendered himself to the dominion of remorse. He was detested by the Protestants, and utterly despised by the Catholics. A bloody sweat, oozing from every pore, crimsoned his bed-clothes. His occasional outcries of remorse and his aspect of misery drove all from his chamber excepting those who were compelled to render him service. He groaned and wept incessantly, exclaiming,

"Oh, what blood! oh, what murders! Alas! why did I follow such evil counsels?"

He saw continually the spectres of the slain, with ghastly, gory wounds, stalking about his bed; and demons of hideous aspect, and with weapons of torture in their hands, with horrid and derisive malice, were impatiently waiting to seize his soul the moment it should pass from the decaying body.

The day before his death he lay for some time upon his bed in perfect silence. Suddenly starting up, he exclaimed,

"Call my brother."

His mother, who was sitting by his side, directed an attendant to call his brother Francis, the Duke of Alençon.

"No, not him," the king replied; "my brother, the King of Navarre, I mean."

Henry of Navarre was then detained in princely imprisonment in the court of Catharine. He had made many efforts to escape, but all had been unavailing.

Catharine directed that Henry should be called. In order to intimidate him, and thus to prevent him from speaking with freedom and boldness to her dying son, she ordered him to be brought through the vaults of the castle, between a double line of armed guards. Henry, as he descended into those gloomy dungeons, and saw the glittering arms of the soldiers, felt that the hour for his assassination had arrived. He, however, passed safely through, and was ushered into the chamber of his brother-in-law and former playfellow, the dying king. Charles IX., subdued by remorse and appalled by approaching death, received him with gentleness and affection, and weeping profusely, embraced him as he knelt by his bedside.

"My brother," said the dying king, "you lose a good master and a good friend. I know that you are not the cause of the troubles which have come upon me. If I had believed all which has been told me, you would not now have been living; but I have always loved you." Then turning his eyes to the queen mother, he said energetically, "Do not trust to--" Here Catharine hastily interrupted him, and prevented the finishing of the sentence with the words "*my mother*."

Charles designated his brother Henry, the King of Poland, as his successor. He expressed the earnest wish that neither his younger brother, Francis, the Duke of Alençon, nor Henry, would disturb the repose of the realm. The next night, as the Cathedral clock was tolling the hour of twelve, the nurse, who was sitting, with two watchers, at the bedside of the dying monarch, heard him sighing and moaning, and then convulsively weeping. Gently she approached the bed and drew aside the curtains. Charles turned his dimmed and despairing eye upon her, and exclaimed,

"Oh, my nurse! my nurse! what blood have I shed! what murders have I committed! Great God! pardon me--pardon me!"

A convulsive shuddering for a moment agitated his frame, his head fell back upon his pillow, and the wretched man was dead. He died at twenty-four years of age, expressing satisfaction that he left no heir to live and to suffer in a world so full of misery. In reference to this guilty king, Chateaubriand says,

"Should we not have some pity for this monarch of twenty-three years, born with fine talents, a taste for literature and the arts, a character naturally generous, whom an execrable mother had tried to deprave by all the abuses of debauchery and power?"

"Yes," warmly responds G. de Felice, "we will have compassion for him, with the Huguenots themselves, whose fathers he ordered to be slain, and who, with a merciful hand, would wipe away the blood which covers his face to find still something human."

Henry, his brother, who was to succeed him upon the throne, was then in Poland. Catharine was glad to have the pusillanimous Charles out of the way. He was sufficiently depraved to commit any crime, without being sufficiently resolute to brave its penalty. Henry III. had, in early life, displayed great vigor of character. At the age of fifteen he had been placed in the command of armies, and in several combats had defeated the veteran generals of the Protestant forces. His renown had extended through Europe, and had contributed much in placing him on the elective throne of Poland. Catharine, by the will of the king, was appointed regent until the return of Henry. She immediately dispatched messengers to recall the King of Poland. In the mean time, she kept Henry of Navarre and her youngest son, the Duke of Alençon, in close captivity, and watched them with the greatest vigilance, that they might make no movements toward the throne.

Henry was by this time utterly weary of his Polish crown, and sighed for the voluptuous pleasures of Paris. The Poles were not willing that their king should leave the realm, as it might lead to civil war in the choice of a successor. Henry was compelled to resort to stratagem to effect his escape. A large and splendid party was invited to the palace. A wilderness of rooms, brilliantly illuminated, were thrown open to the guests. Masked dancers walked the floor in every variety of costume. Wine and wassail filled the halls with revelry. When all were absorbed in music and mirth, the king, by a private passage, stole from the palace, and mounting a swift horse, which was awaiting him in the court-yard, accompanied by two or three friends, commenced his flight from his crown and his Polish throne. Through the long hours of the night they pressed their horses to their utmost speed, and when the morning dawned, obtaining fresh steeds, they hurried on their way, tarrying not for refreshment or repose until they had passed the frontiers of the kingdom. Henry was afraid to take the direct route through the Protestant states of Germany, for the Massacre of St. Bartholomew was still bitterly remembered. He therefore took a circuitous route through Italy, and arrived at Venice in August. In sunny Italy he lingered for some time, surrendering himself to every enervating indulgence, and even bartering the fortresses of France to purchase the luxuries in the midst of which he was reveling. At last, sated with guilty pleasure, he languidly turned his steps toward Paris.

There were now three Henrys, who had been companions in childhood, who were at the head of the three rival houses of Valois, of Bourbon, and of Guise. One of these was King of France. One was King of Navarre. But Henry of Guise was, in wealth and in the attachment of the Catholic population of France, superior to either. The war which ensued is sometimes called *The War of the three Henrys*.

As soon as his mother learned that he was approaching France, she set out from Paris with a magnificent retinue to meet her pet child, taking with her his brother, the Duke of Alençon, and Henry of Navarre. Dissipation had impaired the mental as well as the physical energies of the king, and a maudlin good-nature had absorbed all his faculties. He greeted his brother and his brother-in-law with much kindness, and upon receiving their oaths of obedience, withdrew much of the restraint to which they previously had been subjected. Henry was now known as Henry III. of France. Soon after his coronation he married Louisa of Lorraine, a daughter of one of the sons of the Duke of Guise. She was a pure-minded and lovely woman, and her mild and gentle virtues contrasted strongly with the vulgarity, coarseness, and vice of her degraded husband.

The Duke of Alençon was, however, by no means appeased by the kindness with which he had been received by his brother the king. He called him the robber of his crown, and formed a conspiracy for attacking the carriage of his brother and putting him to death. The plot was revealed to the king. He called his brother to his presence, reproached him with his perfidy and ingratitude, but generously forgave him. But the heart of Alençon was impervious to any appeals of generosity or of honor. Upon the death of Henry III., the Duke of Alençon, his only surviving brother, would ascend the throne.

The Duke of Guise hated with implacable rancor the Duke of Alençon, and even proffered his aid to place Henry of Navarre upon the throne in the event of the death of the king, that he might thus exclude his detested rival. Francis, the Duke of Alençon, was impatient to reach the crown, and again formed a plot to poison his brother. The king was suddenly taken very ill. He declared his brother had poisoned him. As each succeeding day his illness grew more severe, and the probabilities became stronger of its fatal termination, Francis assumed an air of haughtiness and of authority, as if confident that the crown was already his own. The open exultation which he manifested in view of the apparently dying condition of his brother Henry confirmed all in the suspicion that he had caused poison to be administered.

Henry III., believing his death inevitable, called Henry of Navarre to his bedside, and heaping the bitterest invectives upon his brother Francis, urged Henry of Navarre to procure his assassination, and thus secure for himself the vacant throne. Henry of Navarre was the next heir to the throne after the Duke of Alençon, and the dying king most earnestly urged Henry to put the duke to death, showing him the ease with which it could be done, and assuring him that he would be abundantly supported by all the leading nobles of the kingdom. While this scene was taking place at the sick-bed of the monarch, Francis passed through the chamber of his brother without deigning to notice either him or the King of Navarre. Strongly as Henry of Navarre was desirous of securing for himself the throne of France, he was utterly incapable of meditating even upon such a crime, and he refused to give it a second thought.

To the surprise of all, the king recovered, and Francis made no efforts to conceal his disappointment. There were thousands of armed insurgents ready at any moment to rally around the banner of the Duke of Alençon, for they would thus be brought into positions of emolument and power. The king, who was ready himself to act the assassin, treated his assassin-brother with the most profound contempt. No description can convey an adequate idea of the state of France at this time. Universal anarchy prevailed. Civil war, exasperated by the utmost rancor, was raging in nearly all the provinces. Assassinations were continually occurring. Female virtue was almost unknown, and the most shameful licentiousness filled the capital. The treasury was so utterly exhausted that, in a journey made by the king and his retinue in mid-winter, the pages were obliged to sell their cloaks to obtain a bare subsistence. The king, steeped in pollution, a fanatic and a hypocrite, exhibited himself to his subjects bareheaded, barefooted, and half naked, scourging himself with a whip, reciting his prayers, and preparing the way, by the most ostentatious penances, to plunge anew into every degrading sensual indulgence. He was thoroughly despised by his subjects, and many were anxious to exchange him for the reckless and impetuous, but equally depraved Francis.

The situation of the Duke of Alençon was now not only very uncomfortable, but exceedingly perilous. The king did every thing in his power to expose him to humiliations, and was evidently watching for an opportunity to put him to death, either by the dagger or by a cup of poison. The duke, aided by his profligate sister Marguerite, wife of Henry of Navarre, formed a plan for escape.

One dark evening he wrapped himself in a large cloak, and issued forth alone from the Louvre. Passing through obscure streets, he arrived at the suburbs of the city, where a carriage with trusty attendants was in waiting. Driving as rapidly as possible, he gained the open country, and then mounting a very fleet charger, which by previous appointment was provided for him, he spurred his horse at the utmost speed for many leagues, till he met an escort of three hundred men, with whom he took refuge in a fortified town. His escape was not known in the palace until nine o'clock the next morning. Henry was exceedingly agitated when he received the tidings, for he knew that his energetic and reckless brother would join the Protestant party, carrying with him powerful influence, and thus add immeasurably to the distractions which now crowded upon the king.

For once, imminent peril roused Henry III. to vigorous action. He forgot his spaniels, his parrots, his monkeys, and even his painted concubines, and roused himself to circumvent the plans of his hated rival. Letter after letter was sent to all the provinces, informing the governors of the flight of the prince, and commanding the most vigorous efforts to secure his arrest. Francis issued a proclamation declaring the reasons for his escape, and calling upon the Protestants and all who loved the "public good" to rally around him. Hence the short but merciless war which ensued was called "the war of the public good."

The Duke of Alençon was now at the head of a powerful party, for he had thrown himself into the arms of the Protestants, and many of his Catholic partisans followed him. Henry III. called to his aid the fearless and energetic Duke of Guise, and gave him the command of his armies. In the first terrible conflict which ensued Guise was defeated, and received a hideous gash upon his face, which left a scar of which he was very proud as a signet of valor.

Catharine was now in deep trouble. Her two sons were in open arms against each other, heading powerful forces, and sweeping France with whirlwinds of destruction. Henry of Navarre was still detained a prisoner in the French court, though surrounded by all the luxuries and indulgences of the capital. The dignity of his character, and his great popularity, alarmed Catharine, lest, in the turmoil of the times, he should thrust both of her sons from the throne, and grasp the crown himself. Henry and his friends all became fully convinced that Catharine entertained designs upon his life. Marguerite was fully satisfied that it was so, and, bad as she was, as Henry interfered not in the slightest degree with any of her practices, she felt a certain kind of regard for him. The guards who had been assigned to Henry professedly as a mark of honor, and to add to the splendor of his establishment, were in reality his jailers, who watched him with an eagle eye. They were all zealous Papists, and most of them, in the Massacre of St. Bartholomew, had dipped their hands deep in Protestant blood. Catharine watched him with unceasing vigilance, and crowded every temptation upon him which could enervate and ruin. Her depravity did but stimulate her woman's shrewdness and tact.

Henry of Navarre sighed for liberty. He was, however, so closely guarded that escape seemed impossible. At last the following plan was formed for flight. A hunting-party was got up. Henry was to invite persons to attend the chase in whose fidelity he could repose confidence, while one only was to be intrusted with the secret. Others of his friends were secretly to resort to an appointed rendezvous with fresh horses, and all well armed and in sufficient numbers to overpower the guard placed about his person. Henry was to press on in the chase with the utmost eagerness until the horses of the guard were completely exhausted, when his friends with the fresh steeds were to appear, rescue him from the guards, and accompany him in his flight. The guards, being drawn far from the palace, could not speedily obtain fresh horses, neither could they pursue him with their jaded animals.

The Duke of Guise was now in great favor with Henry III. Henry of Navarre, during the few days in which he was making preparation for his flight, blinded the eagle eyes of the duke by affecting great confidence that he should obtain from the king the high office of lieutenant general of France. The duke and Henry III. made themselves very merry over this supposed simplicity of Henry of Navarre, little aware that he was making himself equally merry at their expense.

Two days before the execution of the scheme, a rumor spread through the court that Henry had escaped. For a short time great anxiety and confusion ensued. Henry, being informed of the report and of the agitation which filled the palace, hastened to the apartments where Catharine and the king were in deliberation, and laughingly told them that he had arrested the King of Navarre, and that he now surrendered him to them for safe keeping.

In the morning of the day fixed for his flight, the King of Navarre held a long and familiar conversation with the Duke of Guise, and urged him to accompany him to the hunt. Just as the moment arrived for the execution of the plot, it was betrayed to the king by the treachery of a confederate. Notwithstanding this betrayal, however, matters were so thoroughly arranged that Henry, after several hair-breadth escapes from arrest, accomplished his flight. His apprehension was so great that for sixty miles he rode as rapidly as possible, without speaking a word or stopping for one moment except to mount a fresh horse. He rode over a hundred miles on horseback that day, and took refuge in Alençon, a fortified city held by the Protestants. As soon as his escape was known, thousands of his friends flocked around him.

The Duke of Alençon was not a little troubled at the escape of the King of Navarre, for he was well aware that the authority he had acquired among the Protestants would be lost by the presence of one so much his superior in every respect, and so much more entitled to the confidence of the Protestants. Thus the two princes remained separate, but ready, in case of emergence, to unite their forces, which now amounted to fifty thousand men. Henry of Navarre soon established his head-quarters on the banks of the Loire, where every day fresh parties of Protestants were joining his standard.

Henry III., with no energy of character, despised by his subjects, and without either money or armies, seemed to be now entirely at the mercy of the confederate princes. Henry of Navarre and the Duke of Alençon sent an embassador to the French court to propose terms to Henry III. The King of Navarre required, among other conditions, that France should unite with him in recovering from Spain that portion of the territory of Navarre which had been wrested from his ancestors by Ferdinand and Isabella. While the proposed conditions of peace were under discussion, Catharine succeeded in bribing her son, the Duke of Alençon, to abandon the cause of Henry of Navarre. A treaty of peace was then concluded with the Protestants; and by a royal edict, the full and free exercise of the Protestant religion was guaranteed in every part of France except Paris and a circle twelve miles in diameter around the capital. As a bribe to the Duke of Alençon, he was invested with sovereign power over the three most important provinces of the realm, with an annual income of one hundred thousand crowns. This celebrated treaty, called the *Paix de Monsieur*, because concluded under the auspices of Francis, the brother of the king, was signed at Chastenoy the sixth of May, 1576.

The ambitious and perfidious duke now assumed the title of the Duke of Anjou, and entirely separated himself from the Protestants. He tried to lure the Prince of Condé, the cousin and devoted friend of Henry of Navarre, to accompany him into the town of Bourges. The prince, suspecting treachery, refused the invitation, saying that some rogue would probably be found in the city who would send a bullet through his head.

"The rogue would be hanged, I know," he added, "but the Prince of Condé would be dead. I will not give you occasion, my lord, to hang rogues for love of me."

He accordingly took his leave of the Duke of Alençon, and, putting spurs to his horse, with fifty followers joined the King of Navarre.

Henry was received with royal honors in the Protestant town of Rochelle, where he publicly renounced the Roman Catholic faith, declaring that he had assented to that faith from compulsion, and as the only means of saving his life. He also publicly performed penance for the sin which he declared that he had thus been compelled to commit.

Catharine and Henry III., having detached Francis, who had been the Duke of Alençon, but who was now the Duke of Anjou, from the Protestants, no longer feigned any friendship or even toleration for that cause. They acted upon the principle that no faith was to be kept with heretics. The Protestants, notwithstanding the treaty, were exposed to every species of insult and injury. The Catholics were determined that the Protestant religion should not be tolerated in France, and that all who did not conform to the Church of Rome should either perish or be driven from the kingdom. Many of the Protestants were men of devoted piety, who cherished their religious convictions more tenaciously than life. There were others, however, who joined them merely from motives of political ambition. Though the Protestant party, in France itself, was comparatively small, the great mass of the population being Catholics, yet the party was extremely influential from the intelligence and the rank of its leaders, and from the unconquerable energy with which all of its members were animated.

The weak and irresolute king was ever vacillating between the two parties. The Duke of Guise was the great idol of the Catholics. Henry of Navarre was the acknowledged leader of the Protestants. The king feared them both. It was very apparent that Henry III. could not live long. At his death his brother Francis, Duke of Anjou, would ascend the throne. Should he die childless, Henry of Navarre would be his lawful successor. But the Catholics would be horror-stricken at the idea of seeing a *heretic* on the throne. The Duke of Guise was laying his plans deep and broad to array all the Catholic population of France in his own favor, and thus to rob the Protestant prince of his rights. Henry III., Henry of Navarre, Henry, Duke of Guise, and Francis, Duke of Anjou, had all been playmates in childhood and classmates at school. They were now heading armies, and struggling for the prize of the richest crown in Europe.

Francis was weary of waiting for his brother to die. To strengthen himself, he sought in marriage the hand of Queen Elizabeth of England. Though she had no disposition to receive a husband, she was ever very happy to be surrounded by lovers. She consequently played the coquette with Francis until he saw that there was no probability of the successful termination of his suit. Francis returned to Paris bitterly disappointed, and with new zeal consecrated his sword to the cause of the Catholics. Had Elizabeth accepted his suit, he would then most earnestly have espoused the cause of the Protestants.

Henry III. now determined to make a vigorous effort to crush the Protestant religion. He raised large armies, and gave the command to the Duke of Anjou, the Duke of Guise, and to the brother of the Duke of Guise, the Duke of Mayenne. Henry of Navarre, encountering fearful odds, was welcomed by acclamation to head the small but indomitable band of Protestants, now struggling, not for liberty only, but for life. The king was very anxious to get

Henry of Navarre again in his power, and sent most flattering messages and most pressing invitations to lure him again to his court; but years of captivity had taught a lesson of caution not soon to be forgotten.

Again hideous war ravaged France. The Duke of Anjou, exasperated by disappointed love, disgraced himself by the most atrocious cruelties. He burned the dwellings of the Protestants, surrendered unarmed and defenseless men, and women, and children to massacre. The Duke of Guise, who had inflicted such an ineffaceable stain upon his reputation by the foul murder of the Admiral Coligni, made some atonement for this shameful act by the chivalrous spirit with which he endeavored to mitigate the horrors of civil war.

One day, in the vicinity of Bayonne, a party of Catholics, consisting of a few hundred horse and foot, were conducting to their execution three Protestant young ladies, who, for their faith, were infamously condemned to death. As they were passing over a wide plain, covered with broken woods and heath, they were encountered by a body of Protestants. A desperate battle immediately ensued. The Protestants, impelled by a noble chivalry as well as by religious fervor, rushed upon their foes with such impetuosity that resistance was unavailing, and the Catholics threw down their arms and implored quarter. Many of these soldiers were from the city of Dux. The leader of the Protestant band remembered that at the Massacre of St. Bartholomew all the Protestants in that city had been slain without mercy. With a most deplorable want of magnanimity, he caused all the prisoners who belonged to that place to be separated from the rest, and in cold blood they were slaughtered.

The remainder of the prisoners were from the city of Bayonne, whose inhabitants, though Catholics, had nobly refused to imbrue their hands in the blood of that horrible massacre which Charles IX. had enjoined. To them, after they had seen their comrades surrendered to butchery before their eyes, he restored their horses and their arms, and gave them their entire liberty.

"Go," said he, "to your homes, and there tell the different treatment which I show to soldiers and to assassins."

The three ladies, thus rescued from impending death, were borne back in triumph to their friends. Eight days after this, a trumpet was sounded and a flag of truce appeared emerging from the gates of Bayonne. The friends of the Catholic soldiers who had been thus generously restored sent a beautifully embroidered scarf and a handkerchief to each one of the Protestant soldiers.

KARTINDO PUBLISHING HOUSE (Kartindo.Com)

It is a singular illustration of the blending of the horrors of war and the courtesies of peace, that in the midst of this sanguinary conflict, Henry of Navarre, accompanied by only six companions, accepted an invitation to a fête given by his enemies of the town of Bayonne. He was received with the utmost courtesy. His table was loaded with luxuries. Voluptuous music floated upon the ear; songs and dances animated the festive hours. Henry then returned to head his army and to meet his entertainers in the carnage of the field of battle.

There was but little repose in France during the year 1577. Skirmish succeeded skirmish, and battle was followed by battle; cities were bombarded, villages burned, fields ravaged. All the pursuits of industry were arrested. Ruin, beggary, and woe desolated thousands of once happy homes. Still the Protestants were unsubdued. The king's resources at length were entirely exhausted, and he was compelled again to conclude a treaty of peace. Both parties immediately disbanded their forces, and the blessings of repose followed the discords of war.

One of the Protestant generals, immediately upon receiving the tidings of peace, set out at the utmost speed of his horse to convey the intelligence to Languedoc, where very numerous forces of Protestants and Catholics were preparing for conflict. He spurred his steed over hills and plains till he saw, gleaming in the rays of the morning sun, the banners of the embattled hosts arrayed against each other on a vast plain. The drums and the trumpets were just beginning to sound the dreadful charge which in a few moments would strew that plain with mangled limbs and crimson it with blood. The artillery on the adjoining eminences was beginning to utter its voice of thunder, as balls, more destructive than the fabled bolts of Jove, were thrown into the massive columns marching to the dreadful onset. A few moments later, and the cry, the uproar, and the confusion of the battle would blind every eye and deafen every ear. La Noue, almost frantic with the desire to stop the needless effusion of blood, at the imminent risk of being shot, galloped between the antagonistic armies, waving energetically the white banner of peace, and succeeded in arresting the battle. His generous effort saved the lives of thousands.

Henry III. was required, as a pledge of his sincerity, to place in the hands of the Protestants eight fortified cities. The Reformers were permitted to conduct public worship unmolested in those places only where it was practiced at the time of signing the treaty. In other parts of France they were allowed to retain their belief without persecution, but they were not permitted to meet in any worshiping assemblies. But even these pledges, confirmed by the Edict of Poitiers on the 8th of October, 1577, were speedily broken, like all the rest.

But in the midst of all these conflicts, while every province in France was convulsed with civil war, the king, reckless of the woes of his subjects, rioted in all voluptuous dissipation. He was accustomed to exhibit himself to his court in those effeminate pageants in which he found his only joy, dressed in the flaunting robes of a gay woman, with his bosom open and a string of pearls encircling his neck. On one occasion he gave a fête, when, for the excitement of novelty, the gentlemen, in female robes, were waited upon by the ladies of the court, who were dressed in male attire, or rather undressed, for their persons were veiled by the slightest possible clothing. Such was the corruption of the court of France, and, indeed, of nearly the whole realm in those days of darkness. Domestic purity was a virtue unknown. Law existed only in name. The rich committed any crimes without fear of molestation. In the royal palace itself, one of the favorites of the king, in a paroxysm of anger, stabbed his wife and her waiting-maid while the unfortunate lady was dressing. No notice whatever was taken of this bloody deed. The murderer retained all his offices and honors, and it was the general sentiment of the people of France that the assassination was committed by the order of the sovereign, because the lady refused to be entirely subservient to the wishes of the dissolute king.

CHAPTER VIII

THE LEAGUE

1585-1589

Formation of the league.--Politics in the pulpit.--The League.--Object of the League.--The oath.--Influence of the League.--Its extension.--Vast power of the League.--Alarm of the Protestants.--Adroit measures of Henry III.--Embarrassment of the Leaguers.--Excommunication of Henry IV.--Bold retort.--Edict of Nemours.--Anguish of Henry of Navarre.--Death of Francis.--Redoubled energies.--Toleration.--The challenge.--Efforts to raise an army.--The Leaguers baffled.--The hostile meeting.--Appearance of the two armies.--The charge.--Penitence of Henry of Navarre.--Extraordinary scene.--The battle of Coutras.--The victory.--Exultation of the troops.--Magnanimity of Henry of Navarre.--Conduct of Marguerite.--Court of Henry of Navarre.--Censure by the clergy.--The flying squadron.--Intrigue and gallantry.--Influences used by Catharine.--La Reole.--Treachery of Ussac.--News of the loss of La Reole.--The recapture.--Precarious peace.--Attempt to assassinate Henry.--The assassin humiliated.

About this time there was formed the celebrated league which occupies so conspicuous a position in the history of the sixteenth century. Henry III., though conscious that his throne was trembling beneath him, and courting now the Catholics and again the Protestants, was still amusing himself, day after day, with the most contemptible and trivial vices. The extinction of the house of Valois was evidently and speedily approaching. Henry of Navarre, calm, sagacious, and energetic, was rallying around him all the Protestant influences of Europe, to sustain, in that event, his undeniable claim to the throne. The Duke of Guise, impetuous and fearless, hoped, in successful usurpation, to grasp the rich prize by rallying around his banner all the fanatic energies of Catholic Europe.

Henry III. was alike despised by Catholics and Protestants. His brother Francis, though far more impulsive, had but few traits of character to command respect. He could summon but a feeble band for his support. Henry of Guise was the available candidate for the Catholics. All the priestly influences of France were earnestly combined to advance his claims. They declared that Henry of Navarre had forfeited every shadow of right to the succession by being a heretic. The genealogy of the illustrious house of Guise was blazoned forth, and its descent traced from Charlemagne. It was asserted, and argued in the pulpit and in the camp, that even the house of Valois had usurped the crown which by right belonged to the house of Guise.

Under these circumstances, the most formidable secret society was organized the world has ever known. It assumed the name of The League. Its object was to exterminate Protestantism, and to place the Duke of Guise upon the throne. The following are, in brief, its covenant and oath:

THE LEAGUE

In the name of the Holy Trinity, Father, Son, and Holy Ghost, this League of Catholic princes, lords, and gentlemen shall be instituted to maintain the holy Catholic, apostolical, and Roman Church, abjuring all errors to the contrary. Should opposition to this league arise in any quarter, the associates shall employ all their goods and means, and even their own persons unto death, to punish and hunt down those opposing. Should any of the Leaguers, their associates or friends, be molested, the members of the League shall be bound to employ their bodies, goods, and means to inflict vengeance upon those thus offending. Should any Leaguer, after having taken the oath, withdraw from the association under any pretext whatever, the refractory member shall be injured, in body and goods, in every manner which can be devised, as enemies of God, rebels, and disturbers of the public peace. The Leaguers shall swear implicit obedience to their chief, and shall aid by counsel and service in preserving the League, and in the ruin of all who oppose it. All Catholic towns and villages shall be summoned secretly, by their several governors, to enter into this League, and to furnish arms and men for its execution.

OATH.

I swear by God the Creator, touching the Evangelists, and upon the pain of eternal damnation, that I have entered into this holy Catholic League loyally and sincerely, either to command, to obey, or to serve. I promise, upon my life and honor, to remain in this League to the last drop of my blood, without opposing or retiring upon any pretext whatever.

Such was the character of secret societies in the sixteenth century. A more atrocious confederacy than this the human mind could hardly have conceived.

KARTINDO PUBLISHING HOUSE (Kartindo.Com)

It was, however, peculiarly calculated to captivate the multitude in those days of darkness and blood. Though at first formed and extended secretly, it spread like wildfire through all the cities and provinces of France. Princes, lords, gentlemen, artisans, and peasants rushed into its impious inclosures. The benighted populace, enthralled by the superstitions of the Church, were eager to manifest their zeal for God by wreaking the most awful vengeance upon *heretics*. He who, for any cause, declined entering the League, found himself exposed to every possible annoyance. His house and his barns blazed in midnight conflagrations; his cattle were mutilated and slain; his wife and children were insulted and stoned in the streets. By day and by night, asleep and awake, at home and abroad, at all times and every where, he was annoyed by every conceivable form of injury and violence.

Soon the League became so powerful that no farther secrecy was needful. It stalked abroad in open day, insulting its foes and vaunting its invincibility. The gigantic plan it unblushingly avowed was to exterminate Protestantism by fire and the sword from France; then to drown it in blood in Holland; then to turn to England and purify that kingdom from the taint of heresy; then to march upon Germany; and thus to advance from kingdom to kingdom, in their holy crusade, until Protestantism should be every where ingulfed in blood and flame, and the whole of Europe should be again brought back to the despotism of Rome.

The Duke of Guise was the soul of this mammoth conspiracy, though Philip II., the bigoted King of Spain, was its recorded commander-in-chief. The Protestants were justly alarmed by the enormous energy of the new power thus suddenly evoked against them. The Pope, though at first hostile, soon, with his cardinals, espoused the cause of the League, and consecrated to its support all the weapons which could be wielded by the Vatican. From France, the demoniac organization spread through all the kingdoms of Europe. Hundreds of thousands were arrayed beneath its crimson banner. Even Henry III. in the Louvre, surrounded by his parasites and his concubines, trembled as he saw the shadow of this fearful apparition darkening his court.

He immediately perceived that he must mount the car or be crushed by it. Adroitly he leaped into the seat of the charioteer and seized the reins. The demands of the League he adopted as his own, and urged them with energy. He issued a proclamation commending the League to his subjects, and announcing that he, to set them an example, had signed its covenant and its oath. The Duke of Guise and his followers were quite bewildered by this unexpected step.

The League had demanded the assembling of the States-General, a body somewhat resembling the Congress of the United States. The king immediately summoned them to meet. They declared war against the Protestants. The king adopted the declaration as his own decree, and called loudly for supplies to prosecute the war with vigor. He outleagued the most violent of the Leaguers in denunciations of the Protestants, in declaring that but one religion should be tolerated in France, and in clamoring for arms and munitions of war, that *heresy* might be utterly extirpated. The Leaguers thus found, to their great perplexity, the weapon which they had forged wrested from their hands and wielded against them. They had organized to drive the imbecile Henry III. from the throne. He had seized upon that organization, and was using it to establish himself more firmly there.

The situation of Henry of Navarre was now extremely critical. Pope Sextus V., besides giving the League his Papal blessing, had fulminated against the King of Navarre the awful thunders of excommunication.

The bull of excommunication was exceedingly coarse and vulgar in its denunciatory terms, calling the King of Navarre "*this bastard and detestable progeny of Bourbons.*"

Henry replied to this assault in accents intrepid and resolute, which caused Catholic Europe to stand aghast.

"Henry," said this bold document, "by the grace of God King of Navarre, sovereign prince of Bearn, first peer and prince of France, resists the declaration and excommunication of Sextus V., self-styled Pope of Rome, asserts it to be false, and maintains that Mr. Sextus, the self-styled Pope, *has falsely and maliciously lied;* that he himself is *heretic*, which he will prove in any full and free council lawfully assembled; to which if he does not consent and submit, as he is bound by the canons, he, the King of Navarre, holds and pronounces him to be anti-Christ and heretic, and in that quality declares against him perpetual and irreconcilable war."

This energetic protest was placarded in most of the towns of France, and by some fearless followers of the prince was even attached to the walls of the Vatican. The Pope, though at first much irritated, had the magnanimity to express his admiration of the spirit manifested by Henry.

"There are but two princes in Europe," said he, "to whom I could venture to communicate the grand schemes revolving in my mind, Henry of Navarre and

Elizabeth of England; but, unfortunately, they are both heretics."

Henry III., having no moral principles to guide him in any thing, and having no generous affections of any kind, in carrying out his plan of wielding the energies of the League without any scruples of conscience, issued the infamous Edict of Nemours in 1585, which commanded every Protestant minister to leave the kingdom within one month, and every member of the Reformed faith either to abjure his religion and accept the Catholic faith, or to depart from France within six months. The penalty for disobedience in either of these cases was *death and the confiscation of property*. This edict was executed with great rigor, and many were burned at the stake.

Henry of Navarre was amazed, and, for a time, overwhelmed in receiving the news of this atrocious decree. He clearly foresaw that it must arouse France and all Europe to war, and that a new Iliad of woes was to commence. Leaning his chin upon his hand, he was for a long time lost in profound reverie as he pondered the awful theme. It is said that his anguish was so intense, that when he removed his hand his beard and mustache on that side were turned entirely gray.

But Henry rose with the emergence, and met the crisis with a degree of energy and magnanimity which elicited, in those barbarous times, the admiration even of his enemies. The Protestants heroically grasped their arms and rallied together for mutual protection. War, with all its horrors, was immediately resumed.

Affairs were in this condition when Francis, the Duke of Anjou, was taken sick and suddenly died. This removed another obstruction from the field, and tended to hasten the crisis. Henry III. was feeble, exhausted, and childless. Worn out by shameless dissipation, it was evident to all that he must soon sink into his grave. Who was to be his successor? This was the question, above all others, which agitated France and Europe. Henry of Navarre was, beyond all question, legitimately entitled to the throne; but he was, in the estimation of France, a *heretic*. The League consequently, in view of the impending peril of having a Protestant king, redoubled its energies to exclude him, and to enthrone their bigoted partisan, Henry of Guise. It was a terrific struggle. The Protestants saw suspended upon its issue their property, their religious liberty, their lives, their earthly all. The Catholics were stimulated by all the energies of fanaticism in defense of the Church. All Catholic Europe espoused the one side, all Protestant Europe the other. One single word was enough to arrest all these woes. That word was TOLERATION.

When Henry III. published his famous Edict of Nemours, commanding the conversion, the expulsion, or the death of the Protestants, Henry of Navarre issued another edict replying to the calumnies of the League, and explaining his actions and his motives. Then adopting a step characteristic of the chivalry of the times, he dispatched a challenge to the Duke of Guise, defying him to single combat, or, if he objected to that, to a combat of two with two, ten with ten, or a hundred with a hundred.

"In this challenge," said Henry, "I call Heaven to witness that I am not influenced by any spirit of bravado, but only by the desire of deciding a quarrel which will otherwise cost the lives of thousands."

To this appeal the duke made no reply. It was by no means for his interest to meet on equal terms those whom he could easily outnumber two or three to one.

Though the situation of Henry of Navarre seemed now almost desperate, he maintained his courage and his hope unshaken. His estates were unhesitatingly sold to raise funds. His friends parted with their jewels for gold to obtain the means to carry on the war. But, with his utmost efforts, he could raise an army of but four or five thousand men to resist two armies of twenty thousand each, headed by the Duke of Guise and by his brother, the Duke of Mayenne. Fortunately for Henry, there was but little military capacity in the League, and, notwithstanding their vast superiority in numbers, they were continually circumvented in all their plans by the energy and the valor of the Protestants.

The King of France was secretly rejoiced at the discomfiture of the Leaguers, yet, expressing dissatisfaction with the Duke of Guise, he intrusted the command of the armies to one of his petted favorites, Joyeuse, a rash and fearless youth, who was as prompt to revel in the carnage of the battle-field as in the voluptuousness of the palace. The king knew not whether to choose victory or defeat for his favorite. Victory would increase the influence and the renown of one strongly attached to him, and would thus enable him more successfully to resist the encroachments of the Duke of Guise. Defeat would weaken the overbearing power of the Leaguers, and enable Henry III. more securely to retain his position by the balance of the two rival parties. Joyeuse, ardent and inexperienced, and despising the feeble band he was to encounter, was eager to display his prowess. He pressed eagerly to assail the King of Navarre. The two armies met upon a battle-field a few leagues from Bordeaux. The army of Joyeuse was chiefly of gay and effeminate courtiers and young nobles, who had too much pride to lack courage, but who possessed but little physical vigor, and who were quite unused to the hardships and to the vicissitudes of war.

On the morning of the 20th of October, 1589, as the sun rose over the hills of Perigord, the two armies were facing each other upon the plains of Coutras. The Leaguers were decked with unusual splendor, and presented a glittering array, with gorgeous banners and waving plumes, and uniforms of satin and velvet embroidered by the hands of the ladies of the court. They numbered twelve thousand men. Henry of Navarre, with admirable military skill, had posted his six thousand hardy peasants, dressed in tattered skins, to meet the onset.

And now occurred one of the most extraordinary scenes which history has recorded. It was a source of constant grief to the devout Protestant leaders that Henry of Navarre, notwithstanding his many noble traits of character, was not a man of pure morality. Just before the battle, Du Plessis, a Christian and a hero, approached the King of Navarre and said,

"Sire, it is known to all that you have sinned against God, and injured a respectable citizen of Rochelle by the seduction of his daughter. We can not hope that God will bless our arms in this approaching battle while such a sin remains unrepented of and unrepaired."

The king dismounted from his horse, and, uncovering his head, avowed in the presence of the whole army his sincere grief for what he had done; he called all to witness that he thus publicly implored forgiveness of God, and of the family he had injured, and he pledged his word that he would do every thing in his power to repair the wrong.

The troops were then called to prayers by the ministers. Every man in the ranks fell upon his knees, while one of the clergy implored God to forgive the sin of their chieftain, and to grant them protection and victory.

The strange movement was seen from the Catholic camp. "By death," exclaimed Joyeuse, "the poltroons are frightened. Look! they kneel, imploring our mercy."

"Do not deceive yourself," replied an old captain. "When the Huguenots get into that position, they are ready for hard fighting."

The brilliant battalions of the enemy now began to deploy. Some one spoke of the splendor of their arms. Henry smiled and replied, "We shall have the better aim when the fight begins." Another ventured to intimate that the ministers had rebuked him with needless severity. He replied, "We can not be too humble before God, nor too brave before men." Then turning to his followers, with tears in his eyes, he addressed to them a short and noble speech. He deplored the calamities of war, and solemnly declared that he had drawn arms only in self-defense. "Let them," said he, "perish who are the authors of this war. May the blood shed this day rest upon them alone."

To his two prominent generals, the Prince of Condé and the Count de Soissons, he remarked, with a smile, "To you I shall say nothing but that you are of the house of Bourbon, and, please God, I will show you this day that I am your elder."

The battle almost immediately ensued. Like all fierce fights, it was for a time but a delirious scene of horror, confusion, and carnage. But the Protestants, with sinewy arms, hewed down their effeminate foes, and with infantry and cavalry swept to and fro resistlessly over the plain. The white plume of Henry of Navarre was ever seen waving in the tumultuous throng wherever the battle was waged the fiercest.

There was a singular blending of the facetious with the horrible in this sanguinary scene. Before the battle, the Protestant preachers, in earnest sermons, had compared Henry with David at the head of the Lord's chosen people. In the midst of the bloody fray, when the field was covered with the dying and the dead, Henry grappled one of the standard-bearers of the enemy. At the moment, humorously reminded of the flattering comparison of the preachers, he shouted, with waggery which even the excitement of the battle could not repress,

"Surrender, you uncircumcised Philistine."

In the course of one hour three thousand of the Leaguers were weltering in blood upon the plain, Joyeuse himself, their leader, being among the dead. The defeat of the Catholics was so entire that not more than one fourth of their number escaped from the field of Coutras.

The victors were immediately assembled upon the bloody field, and, after prayers and thanksgiving, they sung, with exultant lips,

KARTINDO PUBLISHING HOUSE (Kartindo.Com)

"The Lord appears my helper now, Nor is my faith afraid What all the sons of earth can do, Since Heaven affords its aid."

Henry was very magnanimous in the hour of victory. When some one asked what terms he should now demand, after so great a discomfiture of his foes, he replied, "*The same as before the battle*."

In reading the records of these times, one is surprised to see how mirth, festivity, and magnificence are blended with blood, misery, and despair. War was desolating France with woes which to thousands of families must have made existence a curse, and yet amid these scenes we catch many glimpses of merriment and gayety. At one time we see Henry III. weeping and groaning upon his bed in utter wretchedness, and again he appears before us reveling with his dissolute companions in the wildest carousals. While Henry of Navarre was struggling with his foes upon the field of battle, Marguerite, his wife, was dancing and flirting with congenial paramours amid all the guilty pleasures of the court. Henry wrote repeatedly for her to come and join him, but she vastly preferred the voluptuousness of the capital to the gloom and the hardships of the Protestant camp. She never loved her husband, and while she wished that he might triumph, and thus confer upon her the illustrious rank of the Queen of France, she still rejoiced in his absence, as it allowed her that perfect freedom which she desired. When she saw indications of approaching peace, she was so apprehensive that she might thus be placed under constraint by the presence of her husband, that she did what she could to perpetuate civil war.

It will be remembered that several of the fortified cities of France were in the hands of the Protestants. Henry of Navarre held his comparatively humble court in the town of Agen, where he was very much beloved and respected by the inhabitants. Though far from irreproachable in his morals, the purity of his court was infinitely superior to that of Henry III. and his mother Catharine. Henry of Navarre was, however, surrounded by a body of gay and light-hearted young noblemen, whose mirth-loving propensities and whose often indecorous festivities he could not control. One evening, at a general ball, these young gentlemen extinguished the lights, and in the darkness a scene of much scandal ensued. Henry was severely censured by the Protestant clergy, and by many others of his friends, for not holding the members of his court in more perfect control. His popularity suffered so severely from this occurrence, that it even became necessary for Henry to withdraw his court from the town.

Catharine and Marguerite, accompanied by a retinue of the most voluptuously-beautiful girls of France, set out to visit the court of Henry of Navarre, which had been transferred to Neruc. Henry, hearing of their approach, placed himself at the head of five hundred gentlemen, and hastened to meet his mother-in-law and his wife, with their characteristic and congenial train. These were the instrumentalities with which Catharine and Marguerite hoped to bend the will of Henry and his friends to suit their purposes. Catharine had great confidence in the potency of the influence which these pliant maidens could wield, and they were all instructed in the part which they were to act. She was accustomed to call these allies her *flying squadron*.

There then ensued a long series of negotiations, intermingled with mirth, gallantry, and intrigue, but the result of which was a treaty highly conducive to the interests of the Protestants. Various places were designated where their religion should be freely tolerated, and in which they were to be allowed to build conventicles. They were also permitted to raise money for the support of their ministers, and fourteen cities were surrendered to their government. Several incidents occurred during these negotiations very characteristic of the corrupt manners of the times.

Marguerite devoted herself most energetically to the promotion of the success of Henry's plans. Catharine found herself, notwithstanding all her artifice, and all the peculiar seductions of her female associates, completely foiled by the sagacity and the firmness of Henry. She had brought with her Monsieur de Pibrac, a man very celebrated for his glowing eloquence and for his powers of persuasion. The oratory of Pibrac, combined with the blandishments of the ladies, were those co-operative influences which the queen imagined none would be able to resist. Marguerite, however, instructed in the school of Catharine, succeeded in obtaining entire control over the mind of Pibrac himself, and he became a perfect tool in her hands. Catharine, thus foiled, was compelled to grant far more favorable terms to the Protestants than she had contemplated.

La Reole was one of the towns of security surrendered to the Protestants. There was, however, so little of good faith in that day, that, notwithstanding the pledge of honor, possession of the place could only be retained by vigilance. The government of the town had been conferred upon a veteran Protestant general by the name of Ussac. His days, from early youth, had been passed on fields of battle. He was now far advanced in years, in feeble health, and dreadfully disfigured by wounds received in the face. One of the most fascinating of the ladies of the queen-mother lavished such endearments upon the old man, already in his dotage, that he lost his principles and all self-control, and made himself very ridiculous by assuming the airs of a young lover. Henry had the imprudence to join in the mockery with which the court regarded his tenderness. This was an indignity which an old man could never forget. Instigated by his beautiful seducer, he became entirely unmindful of those principles of honor which had embellished his life, and in revenge invited a Roman Catholic general to come and take possession of the town.

Henry was informed of this act of treachery while dancing at a very brilliant entertainment given in his palace. He quietly whispered to Turenne, Sully, and a few others of his most intimate friends, requesting them to escape from the room, gather around them such armed men as they could, and join him at a rendezvous in the country. They all stole unperceived from the mirthful party, concealed their swords beneath their cloaks, traveled all night, and arrived, just as the day began to dawn, before the gates of the city. They found the place, as they had expected, entirely unprepared for such a sudden attack, and, rushing in, regained it without difficulty. The Catholic soldiers retreated to the castle, where they held out a few days, and many of them perished in the assault by which it was soon taken.

Such was the character of the nominal peace which now existed. A partisan warfare was still continued throughout France. Catharine and her maids did every thing in their power to excite dissensions between the Protestant leaders. In this they succeeded so well that the Prince of Condé became so exasperated against Turenne as to challenge him to single combat.

Such a peace as we have above described could not, of course, be lasting. Both parties were soon again gathering all their forces for war. There is a tedious monotony in the recital of the horrors of battle. Cities bombarded, and sacked, and burned; shells exploding in the cradle of infancy and in the chambers of mothers and maidens; mutilated bodies trampled beneath the hoofs of horses; the cry of the maddened onset, the shrieks of the wounded, and the groans of the dying; the despair of the widow and the orphan; smouldering ruins of once happy homes; the fruits of the husbandman's toils trodden into the mire; starvation, misery, and death--these are ever the fruits of war.

During the short interval of peace, many attempts had been made to assassinate Henry of Navarre by the partisans of the Duke of Guise. Henry was, one fine morning, setting out with a few friends for a ride of pleasure. Just as the party were leaving the court-yard, he was informed that an assassin, very powerfully mounted, was prepared to meet him on the way and to take his life. Henry apparently paid no heed to the warning, but rode along conversing gayly with his friends. They soon met, in a retired part of the way, a stranger, armed according to the custom of the times, and mounted upon a very magnificent steed, which had been prepared for him to facilitate his escape after the accomplishment of the fell deed. Henry immediately rode up to the assassin, addressed him in terms of great familiarity and cordiality, and, professing to admire the beautiful charger upon which he was mounted, requested him to dismount, that he might try the splendid animal. The man, bewildered, obeyed the wishes of the king, when Henry leaped into the saddle, and, seizing the two loaded pistols at the saddle-bow, looked the man sternly in the eye, and said,

"I am told that you seek to kill me. You are now in my power, and I could easily put you to death; but I will not harm you."

He then discharged the two pistols in the air, and permitted the humiliated man to mount his horse and ride away unharmed.

CHAPTER IX

THE ASSASSINATION OF THE DUKE OF GUISE AND OF HENRY III

1589

Imbecility of the king.--Haughtiness of the Duke of Guise.--The duke goes to Paris.--Interview with the king.--Two rival courts.--The Swiss guard defeated.--Tumult in the city.--Dignity of Achille de Harlai.--Measures adopted by the duke.--Endeavors to obtain an assassin.--The king at Blois.--Assassination of the Duke of Guise.--Interview between the king and Catharine.--Indignation of the League.--Anathemas against the king.--The king seeks aid from the Protestants.--Desolations of war.--Compact with Henry of Navarre.--Interview at Plessis les Tours.--The manifesto.--Renewed war.--Duchess of Montpensier.--The flag of truce.--Assassination of Henry III.--Arrival of Henry of Navarre.--Dying scene.--Henry IV. assumes the crown.--Difficulties of the new reign.--Danger of assassination.--Religious principles of Henry IV.--News of the death of Henry III.--Abandoned by the Catholics.--The retreat.--The stand at Dieppe.--Henry urged to fly to England.--Anecdote.--Arrival of the fleet from England.--Bigotry of the Catholics.--Desolation of France.--Ignoble conduct of the League.--Paris besieged.--Assault of Etampes.--Letter from Lorraine.--Military reprisals.--Activity of Henry.--Dissension among the Leaguers.--Triumphant progress of Henry.--Wonderful escape.

The war, again resumed, was fiercely prosecuted. Henry III. remained most of the time in the gilded saloons of the Louvre, irritable and wretched, and yet incapable of any continued efficient exertion. Many of the zealous Leaguers, indignant at the pusillanimity he displayed, urged the Duke of Guise to dethrone Henry III. by violence, and openly to declare himself King of France. They assured him that the nation would sustain him by their arms. But the duke was not prepared to enter upon so bold a measure, as he hoped that the death of the king would soon present to him a far more favorable opportunity for the assumption of the throne. Henry III. was in constant fear that the duke, whose popularity in France was almost boundless, might supplant him, and he therefore forbade him to approach the metropolis.

KARTINDO PUBLISHING HOUSE (Kartindo.Com)

Notwithstanding this prohibition, the haughty duke, accompanied by a small party of his intrepid followers, as if to pay court to his sovereign, boldly entered the city. The populace of the capital, ever ripe for excitement and insurrection, greeted him with boundless enthusiasm. Thousands thronged the broad streets through which he passed with a small but brilliant retinue. Ladies crowded the windows, waving scarfs, cheering him with smiles, and showering flowers at his feet. The cry resounded along the streets, penetrating even the apartments of the Louvre, and falling appallingly upon the ear of the king:

"Welcome--welcome, great duke. Now you are come, we are safe."

Henry III. was amazed and terrified by this insolence of his defiant subject. In bewilderment, he asked those about him what he should do.

"Give me the word," said a colonel of his guard, "and I will plunge my sword through his body."

"Smite the shepherd," added one of the king's spiritual counselors, "and the sheep will disperse."

But Henry feared to exasperate the populace of Paris by the assassination of a noble so powerful and so popular. In the midst of this consultation, the Duke of Guise, accompanied by the queen-mother Catharine, whom he had first called upon, entered the Louvre, and, passing through the numerous body-guard of the king, whom he saluted with much affability, presented himself before the feeble monarch. The king looked sternly upon him, and, without any word of greeting, exclaimed angrily,

"Did I not forbid you to enter Paris?"

"Sire," the duke replied, firmly, but with affected humility, "I came to demand justice, and to reply to the accusations of my enemies."

The interview was short and unrelenting. The king, exasperated almost beyond endurance, very evidently hesitated whether to give the signal for the immediate execution of his dreaded foe. There were those at his side, with arms in their hands, who were eager instantly to obey his bidding. The Duke of Guise perceived the imminence of his danger, and, feigning sudden indisposition, immediately retired. In his own almost regal mansion he gathered around him his followers and his friends, and thus placed himself in a position where even the arm of the sovereign could not venture to touch him.

There were now in Paris, as it were, two rival courts, emulating each other in splendor and power. The one was that of the king at the Louvre, the other was that of the duke in his palace. It was rumored that the duke was organizing a conspiracy to arrest the king and hold him a captive. Henry III., to strengthen his body-guard, called a strong force of Swiss mercenaries into the city. The retainers of the duke, acting under the secret instigation of their chieftain, roused the populace of Paris to resist the Swiss. Barricades were immediately constructed by filling barrels with stones and earth; chains were stretched across the streets from house to house; and organized bands, armed with pikes and muskets, threatened even the gates of the Louvre.

A conflict soon ensued, and the Swiss guard were defeated by the mob at every point. The Duke of Guise, though he secretly guided all these movements, remained in his palace, affecting to have no share in the occurrences. Night came. Confusion and tumult rioted in the city. The insurgent populace, intoxicated and maddened, swarmed around the walls of the palace, and the king was besieged. The spiritless and terrified monarch, disguising himself in humble garb, crept to his stables, mounted a fleet horse, and fled from the city. Riding at full speed, he sought refuge in Chartres, a walled town forty miles southeast of Paris.

The flight of the king before an insurgent populace was a great victory to the duke. He was thus left in possession of the metropolis without any apparent act of rebellion on his own part, and it became manifestly his duty to do all in his power to preserve order in the capital thus surrendered to anarchy. The duke had ever been the idol of the populace, but now nearly the whole population of Paris, and especially the influential citizens, looked to him as their only protector.

Some, however, with great heroism, still adhered to the cause of the king. The Duke of Guise sent for Achille de Harlai, President of the Council, and endeavored to win him over to his cause, that he might thus sanction his usurpation by legal forms; but De Harlai, fixing his eyes steadfastly upon the duke, fearlessly said,

"'Tis indeed pitiable when the valet expels his master. As for me, my soul belongs to my Maker, and my fidelity belongs to the king. My body alone is in the hands of the wicked. You talk of assembling the Parliament. When the majesty of the prince is violated, the magistrate is without authority." The intrepid president was seized and imprisoned.

The followers of Henry III. soon gathered around him at Chartres, and he fortified himself strongly there. The Duke of Guise, though still protesting great loyalty, immediately assumed at Paris the authority of a sovereign. He assembled around him strong military forces, professedly to protect the capital from disturbance. For a month or two negotiations were conducted between the two parties for a compromise, each fearing the other too much to appeal to the decisions of the sword. At last Henry III. agreed to appoint the Duke of Guise lieutenant general of France and high constable of the kingdom. He also, while pledging himself anew to wage a war of extermination against the Protestants, promised to bind the people of France, by an oath, to exclude from the succession to the throne all persons suspected even of Protestantism. This would effectually cut off the hopes of Henry of Navarre, and secure the crown to the Duke of Guise upon the death of the king.

Both of the antagonists now pretended to a sincere reconciliation, and Henry, having received Guise at Chartres with open arms, returned to Paris, meditating how he might secure the death of his dreaded and powerful rival. Imprisonment was not to be thought of, for no fortress in France could long hold one so idolized by the populace. The king applied in person to one of his friends, a brave and honest soldier by the name of Crillon, to assassinate the duke.

"I am not an executioner," the soldier proudly replied, "and the function does not become my rank. But I will challenge the duke to open combat, and will cheerfully sacrifice my life that I may take his."

This plan not meeting with the views of the king, he applied to one of the commanders of his guard named Lorgnac. This man had no scruples, and with alacrity undertook to perform the deed. Henry, having retired to the castle of Blois, about one hundred miles south of Paris, arranged all the details, while he was daily, with the most consummate hypocrisy, receiving his victim with courteous words and smiles. The king summoned a council to attend him in his cabinet at Blois on the 23d of December. It was appointed at an early hour, and the Duke of Guise attended without his usual retinue. He had been repeatedly warned to guard against the treachery of Henry, but his reply was,

[Illustration: ASSASSINATION OF HENRY, DUKE OF GUISE.]

"I do not know that man on earth who, hand to hand with me, would not have his full share of fear. Besides, I am always so well attended that it would not be easy to find me off my guard."

The duke arrived at the door of the cabinet after passing through long files of the king's body-guard. Just as he was raising the tapestry which veiled the entrance, Lorgnac sprang upon him and plunged a dagger into his throat. Others immediately joined in the assault, and the duke dropped, pierced with innumerable wounds, dead upon the floor.

Henry, hearing the noise and knowing well what it signified, very coolly stepped from his cabinet into the ante-chamber, and, looking calmly upon the bloody corpse, said,

"Do you think he is dead, Lorgnac?"

"Yes, sire," Lorgnac replied, "he looks like it."

"Good God, how tall he is!" said the king. "He seems taller dead than when he was living." Then giving the gory body a kick, he exclaimed, "Venomous beast, thou shalt cast forth no more venom."

In the same manner the duke had treated the remains of the noble Admiral Coligni, a solemn comment upon the declaration, "With what measure ye mete it shall be measured to you again."

Cardinal Guise, the brother of the duke, was immediately arrested by order of the king, and sent to prison, where he was assassinated. Henry III. soon after repaired to the bedside of Catharine his mother, who was lying sick in one of the chambers of the castle. Nothing can show more clearly the character of the times and of the personages than the following laconic dialogue which ensued:

"How do you do, mother, this morning?" inquired the king.

"I am better than I have been," she replied.

"So am I," Henry rejoined, gayly, "for I have made myself this morning King of France by putting to death the King of Paris."

KARTINDO PUBLISHING HOUSE (Kartindo.Com)

"Take care," this hardened woman exclaimed, "that you do not soon find yourself *king of nothing*. Diligence and resolution are now absolutely necessary for you."

She then turned upon her pillow without the slightest apparent emotion. In twelve days from this time, this wretched queen, deformed by every vice, without one single redeeming virtue, breathed her last, seventy years of age. She was despised by the Catholics, and hated by the Protestants.

These acts of violence and crime roused the League to the most intense energy. The murder of the Duke of Guise, and especially the murder of his brother, a cardinal in the Church, were acts of impiety which no atonement could expiate. Though Henry was a Catholic, and all his agents in these atrocious murders were Catholics, the death of the Duke of Guise increased vastly the probability that Protestant influences might become dominant at court. The Pope issued a bull of excommunication against all who should advocate the cause of Henry III. The Sorbonne published a decree declaring that the king had forfeited all right to the obedience of his subjects, and justifying them in taking up arms against him. The clergy, from the pulpit, refused communion, absolution, and burial in holy ground to every one who yielded obedience to "the perfidious apostate and tyrant; Henry of Valois."

The League immediately chose the Duke of Mayenne, a surviving brother of the Duke of Guise, as its head. The Pope issued his anathemas against Henry III., and Spain sent her armies to unite with the League. Henry now found it necessary to court the assistance of the Protestants. He dreaded to take this step, for he was superstitious in the extreme, and he could not endure the thought of any alliance with heretics. He had still quite a formidable force which adhered to him, for many of the highest nobles were disgusted with the arrogance of the Guises, and were well aware that the enthronement of the house of Guise would secure their own banishment from court.

The triumph of the League would be total discomfiture to the Protestants. No freedom of worship or of conscience whatever would be allowed them. It was therefore for the interest of the Protestants to sustain the more moderate party hostile to the League. It was estimated that about one sixth of the inhabitants of France were at that time Protestants.

Wretched, war-scathed France was now distracted by three parties. First, there were the Protestants, contending only in self-defense against persecution, and yet earnestly praying that, upon the death of the king, Henry of Navarre, the legitimate successor, might ascend the throne. Next came those Catholics who were friendly to the claims of Henry from their respect for the ancient law of succession. Then came, combined in the League, the bigoted partisans of the Church, resolved to exterminate from Europe, with fire and sword, the detested heresy of Protestantism.

Henry III. was now at the castle of Blois. Paris was hostile to him. The Duke of Mayenne, younger brother of the Duke of Guise, at the head of five thousand soldiers of the League, marched to the metropolis, where he was received by the Parisians with unbounded joy. He was urged by the populace and the Parliament in Paris to proclaim himself king. But he was not yet prepared for so decisive a step.

No tongue can tell the misery which now pervaded ill-fated France. Some cities were Protestant, some were Catholic; division, and war, and blood were every where. Armed bands swept to and fro, and conflagration and slaughter deluged the kingdom.

The king immediately sent to Henry of Navarre, promising to confer many political privileges upon the Protestants, and to maintain Henry's right to the throne, if he would aid him in the conflict against the League. The terms of reconciliation were soon effected. Henry of Navarre, then leaving his army to advance by rapid marches, rode forward with his retinue to meet his brother-in-law, Henry of Valois. He found him at one of the ancient palaces of France, Plessis les Tours. The two monarchs had been friends in childhood, but they had not met for many years. The King of Navarre was urged by his friends not to trust himself in the power of Henry III. "For," said they, "the King of France desires nothing so much as to obtain reconciliation with the Pope, and no offering can be so acceptable to the Pope as the death of a heretic prince."

Henry hesitated a moment when he arrived upon an eminence which commanded a distant view of the palace. Then exclaiming, "God guides me, and He will go with me," he plunged his spurs into his horse's side, and galloped forward.

The two monarchs met, each surrounded with a gorgeous retinue, in one of the magnificent avenues which conducted to the castle. Forgetting the animosities of years, and remembering only the friendships of childhood, they cast themselves cordially into each other's arms. The multitude around rent the air

KARTINDO PUBLISHING HOUSE (Kartindo.Com)

with their acclamations.

Henry of Navarre now addressed a manifesto to all the inhabitants of France in behalf of their woe-stricken country. "I conjure you all," said he, "Catholics as well as Protestants, to have pity on the state and on yourselves. We have all done and suffered evil enough. We have been four years intoxicate, insensate, and furious. Is not this sufficient? Has not God smitten us all enough to allay our fury, and to make us wise at last?"

But passion was too much aroused to allow such appeals to be heeded. Battle after battle, with ever-varying success, ensued between the combined forces of the king and Henry of Navarre on one side, and of the League, aided by many of the princes of Catholic Europe, on the other. The storms of winter swept over the freezing armies and the smouldering towns, and the wail of the victims of horrid war blended with the moanings of the gale. Spring came, but it brought no joy to desolate, distracted, wretched France. Summer came, and the bright sun looked down upon barren fields, and upon a bleeding, starving, fighting nation. Henry of Navarre, in command of the royal forces, at the head of thirty thousand troops, was besieging Paris, which was held by the Duke of Mayenne, and boldly and skillfully was conducting his approaches to a successful termination. The cause of the League began to wane. Henry III. had taken possession of the castle of St. Cloud, and from its elevated windows looked out with joy upon the bold assaults and the advancing works.

[Illustration: THE ASSASSINATION OF HENRY III.]

The leaders of the League now resolved to resort again to the old weapon of assassination. Henry III. was to be killed. But no man could kill him unless he was also willing to sacrifice his own life. The Duchess of Montpensier, sister of the Duke of Guise, for the accomplishment of this purpose, won the love, by caressings and endearments, of Jaques Clement, an ardent, enthusiastic monk of wild and romantic imaginings, and of the most intense fanaticism. The beautiful duchess surrendered herself without any reserve whatever to the paramour she had enticed to her arms, that she might obtain the entire supremacy over his mind. Clement concealed a dagger in his bosom, and then went out from the gates of the city accompanied by two soldiers and with a flag of truce, ostensibly to take a message to the king. He refused to communicate his message to any one but the monarch himself. Henry III., supposing it to be a communication of importance, perhaps a proposition to surrender, ordered him to be admitted immediately to his cabinet. Two persons only were present with the king. The monk entered, and, kneeling, drew a letter from the sleeve of his gown, presented it to the king, and instantly drawing a large knife from its concealment, plunged it into the entrails of his victim. The king uttered a piercing cry, caught the knife from his body and struck at the head of his murderer, wounding him above the eye. The two gentlemen who were present instantly thrust their swords through the body of the assassin, and he fell dead.

The king, groaning with anguish, was undressed and borne to his bed. The tidings spread rapidly, and soon reached the ears of the King of Navarre, who was a few miles distant at Meudon. He galloped to St. Cloud, and knelt with gushing tears at the couch of the dying monarch. Henry III. embraced him with apparently the most tender affection. In broken accents, interrupted with groans of anguish, he said,

"If my wound proves mortal, I leave my crown to you as my legitimate successor. If my will can have any effect, the crown will remain as firmly upon your brow as it was upon that of Charlemagne."

He then assembled his principal officers around him, and enjoined them to unite for the preservation of the monarchy, and to sustain the claims of the King of Navarre as the indisputable heir to the throne of France.

A day of great anxiety passed slowly away, and as the shades of evening settled down over the palace, it became manifest to all that the wound was mortal. The wounded monarch writhed upon his bed in fearful agony. At midnight, Henry of Navarre, who was busily engaged superintending some of the works of the siege, was sent for, as the King of France was dying. Accompanied by a retinue of thirty gentlemen, he proceeded at full speed to the gates of the castle where the monarch was struggling in the grasp of the King of Terrors.

It is difficult to imagine the emotions which must have agitated the soul of Henry of Navarre during this dark and gloomy ride. The day had not yet dawned when he arrived at the gates of the castle. The first tidings he received were, *The king is dead*. It was the 2d of August, 1589.

Henry of Navarre was now Henry IV., King of France. But never did monarch ascend the throne under circumstances of greater perplexity and peril. Never was a more distracted kingdom placed in the hands of a new monarch. Henry was now thirty-four years of age. The whole kingdom was convulsed by warring factions. For years France had been desolated by all the most virulent elements of religious and political animosity. All hearts were demoralized by

KARTINDO PUBLISHING HOUSE (Kartindo.Com)

familiarity with the dagger of the assassin and the carnage of the battle-field. Almost universal depravity had banished all respect for morality and law. The whole fabric of society was utterly disorganized.

Under these circumstances, Henry developed that energy and sagacity which have given him a high position among the most renowned of earthly monarchs. He immediately assembled around him that portion of the royal army in whose fidelity he could confide. Without the delay of an hour, he commenced dictating letters to all the monarchies of Europe, announcing his accession to the throne, and soliciting their aid to confirm him in his legitimate rights.

As the new sovereign entered the chamber of the deceased king, he found the corpse surrounded by many of the Catholic nobility of France. They were ostentatiously solemnizing the obsequies of the departed monarch. He heard many low mutterings from these zealous partisans of Rome, that they would rather die a thousand deaths than allow a Protestant king to ascend the throne. Angry eyes glared upon him from the tumultuous and mutinous crowd, and, had not Henry retired to consult for his own safety, he also might have fallen the victim of assassination. In the intense excitement of these hours, the leading Catholics held a meeting, and appointed a committee to wait upon Henry, and inform him that he must immediately abjure Protestantism and adopt the Catholic faith, or forfeit their support to the crown.

"Would you have me," Henry replied, "profess conversion with the dagger at my throat? And could you, in the day of battle, follow one with confidence who had thus proved that he was an apostate and without a God? I can only promise carefully to examine the subject that I may be guided to the truth."

Henry was a Protestant from the force of circumstances rather than from conviction. He was not a theologian either in mind or heart, and he regarded the Catholics and Protestants merely as two political parties, the one or the other of which he would join, according as, in his view, it might promote his personal interests and the welfare of France. In his childhood he was a Catholic. In boyhood, under the tuition of his mother, Protestant influences were thrown around him, and he was nominally a Protestant. He saved his life at St. Bartholomew by avowing the Catholic faith. When he escaped from the Catholic court and returned to his mother's Protestant court in Navarre, he espoused with new vigor the cause of his Protestant friends. These changes were of course more or less mortifying, and they certainly indicated a total want of religious conviction. He now promised carefully to look at the arguments on both sides of the question, and to choose deliberately that which

KARTINDO PUBLISHING HOUSE (Kartindo.Com)

should seem to him right. This arrangement, however, did not suit the more zealous of the Catholics, and, in great numbers, they abandoned his camp and passed over to the League.

The news of the death of Henry III. was received with unbounded exultation in the besieged city. The Duchess of Montpensier threw her arms around the neck of the messenger who brought her the welcome tidings, exclaiming,

"Ah! my friend, is it true? Is the monster really dead? What a gratification! I am only grieved to think that he did not know that it was I who directed the blow."

She rode out immediately, that she might have the pleasure herself of communicating the intelligence. She drove through the streets, shouting from her carriage, "Good news! good news! the tyrant is dead." The joy of the priests rose to the highest pitch of fanatical fervor. The assassin was even canonized. The Pope himself condescended to pronounce a eulogium upon the "*martyr*," and a statue was erected to his memory, with the inscription, "St. Jaques Clement, pray for us."

The League now proclaimed as king the old Cardinal of Bourbon, under the title of Charles X., and nearly all of Catholic Europe rallied around this pretender to the crown. No one denied the validity of the title, according to the principles of legitimacy, of Henry IV. His rights, however, the Catholics deemed forfeited by his Protestant tendencies. Though Henry immediately issued a decree promising every surety and support to the Catholic religion as the established religion of France, still, as he did not also promise to devote all his energies to the extirpation of the heresy of Protestantism, the great majority of the Catholics were dissatisfied.

Epernon, one of the most conspicuous of the Catholic leaders, at the head of many thousand Catholic soldiers, waited upon the king immediately after the death of Henry III., and informed him that they could not maintain a Protestant on the throne. With flying banners and resounding bugles they then marched from the camp and joined the League. So extensive was this disaffection, that in one day Henry found himself deserted by all his army except six thousand, most of whom were Protestants. Nearly thirty thousand men had abandoned him, some to retire to their homes, and others to join the enemy.

The army of the League within the capital was now twenty thousand strong.

They prepared for a rush upon the scattered and broken ranks of Henry IV. Firmly, fearlessly, and with well matured plans, he ordered a prompt retreat. Catholic Europe aroused itself in behalf of the League. Henry appealed to Protestant Europe to come to his aid. Elizabeth of England responded promptly to his appeal, and promised to send a fleet and troops to the harbor of Dieppe, about one hundred miles northwest of Paris, upon the shores of the English Channel. Firmly, and with concentrated ranks, the little army of Protestants crossed the Seine. Twenty thousand Leaguers eagerly pursued them, watching in vain for a chance to strike a deadly blow. Henry ate not, slept not, rested not. Night and day, day and night, he was every where present, guiding, encouraging, protecting this valiant band. Planting a rear guard upon the western banks of the Seine, the chafing foe was held in check until the Royalist army had retired beyond the Oise. Upon the farther banks of this stream Henry again reared his defenses, thwarting every endeavor of his enemies, exasperated by such unexpected discomfiture.

As Henry slowly retreated toward the sea, all the Protestants of the region through which he passed, and many of the moderate Catholics who were in favor of the royal cause and hostile to the house of Guise, flocked to his standard. He soon found himself, with seven thousand very determined men, strongly posted behind the ramparts of Dieppe.

But the Duke of Mayenne had also received large accessions. The spears and banners of his proud host, now numbering thirty-five thousand, gleamed from all the hills and valleys which surrounded the fortified city. For nearly a month there was almost an incessant conflict. Every morning, with anxious eyes, the Royalists scanned the watery horizon, hoping to see the fleet of England coming to their aid. Cheered by hope, they successfully beat back their assailants. The toils of the king were immense. With exalted military genius he guided every movement, at the same time sharing the toil of the humblest soldier. "It is a marvel," he wrote, "how I live with the labor I undergo. God have pity upon me, and show me mercy."

Some of Henry's friends, appalled by the strength of the army pursuing them, urged him to embark and seek refuge in England.

"Here we are," Henry replied, "in France, and here let us be buried. If we fly now, all our hopes will vanish with the wind which bears us."

In a skirmish, one day, one of the Catholic chieftains, the Count de Bélin, was taken captive. He was led to the head-quarters of the king. Henry greeted him with perfect cordiality, and, noticing the astonishment of the count in seeing but a few scattered soldiers where he had expected to see a numerous army, he said, playfully, yet with a confident air,

"You do not perceive all that I have with me, M. de Bélin, for you do not reckon God and the right on my side."

The indomitable energy of Henry, accompanied by a countenance ever serene and cheerful under circumstances apparently so desperate, inspired the soldiers with the same intrepidity which glowed in the bosom of their chief.

But at last the valiant little band, so bravely repelling overwhelming numbers, saw, to their inexpressible joy, the distant ocean whitened with the sails of the approaching English fleet. Shouts of exultation rolled along their exhausted lines, carrying dismay into the camp of the Leaguers. A favorable wind pressed the fleet rapidly forward, and in a few hours, with streaming banners, and exultant music, and resounding salutes, echoed and re-echoed from English ships and French batteries, the fleet of Elizabeth, loaded to its utmost capacity with money, military supplies, and men, cast anchor in the little harbor of Dieppe.

Nearly six thousand men, Scotch and English, were speedily disembarked. The Duke of Mayenne, though his army was still double that of Henry IV., did not dare to await the onset of his foes thus recruited. Hastily breaking up his encampment, he retreated to Paris. Henry IV., in gratitude to God for the succor which he had thus received from the Protestant Queen of England, directed that thanksgivings should be offered in his own quarters according to the religious rites of the Protestant Church. This so exasperated the Catholics, even in his own camp, that a mutiny was excited, and several of the Protestant soldiers were wounded in the fray. So extreme was the fanaticism at this time that, several Protestants, after a sanguinary fight, having been buried on the battle-field promiscuously in a pit with some Catholics who had fallen by their side, the priests, even of Henry's army, ordered the Protestant bodies to be dug up and thrown out as food for dogs.

While these scenes were transpiring in the vicinity of Dieppe, almost every part of France was scathed and cursed by hateful war. Every province, city, village, had its partisans for the League or for the king. Beautiful France was as a volcano in the world of woe, in whose seething crater flames, and blood, and

KARTINDO PUBLISHING HOUSE (Kartindo.Com)

slaughter, the yell of conflict and the shriek of agony, blended in horrors which no imagination can compass. There was an end to every earthly joy. Cities were bombarded, fields of grain trampled in the mire, villages burned. Famine rioted over its ghastly victims. Hospitals were filled with miserable multitudes, mutilated and with festering wounds, longing for death. Not a ray of light pierced the gloom of this dark, black night of crime and woe. And yet, undeniably, the responsibility before God must rest with the League. Henry IV. was the lawful king of France. The Catholics had risen in arms to resist his rights, because they feared that he would grant liberty of faith and worship to the Protestants.

The League adopted the most dishonorable and criminal means to alienate from Henry the affections of the people. They forged letters, in which the king atrociously expressed joy at the murder of Henry III., and declared his determination by dissimulation and fraud to root out Catholicism entirely from France. No efforts of artifice were wanting to render the monarch odious to the Catholic populace. Though the Duke of Mayenne occasionally referred to the old Cardinal of Bourbon as the king whom he acknowledged, he, with the characteristic haughtiness of the family of Guise, assumed himself the air and the language of a sovereign. It was very evident that he intended to place himself upon the throne.

Henry IV., with the money furnished by Elizabeth, was now able to pay his soldiers their arrears. His army steadily increased, and he soon marched with twenty-three thousand troops and fourteen pieces of artillery to lay siege to Paris. His army had unbounded confidence in his military skill. With enthusiastic acclamations they pursued the retreating insurgents. Henry was now on the offensive, and his troops were posted for the siege of Paris, having driven the foe within its walls. After one sanguinary assault, the king became convinced that he had not with him sufficient force to carry the city. The Duke of Mayenne stood firmly behind the intrenchments of the capital, with an army much strengthened by re-enforcements of Spanish and Italian troops. Henry accordingly raised the siege, and marched rapidly to Etampes, some forty miles south of Paris, where a large part of his foes had established themselves. He suddenly attacked the town and carried it by assault. The unhappy inhabitants of this city had, in the course of four months, experienced the horrors of three assaults. The city, in that short period, had been taken and retaken three times.

While at Etampes, Henry received a letter from the beautiful but disconsolate Louisa of Lorraine, the widow of Henry III., imploring him to avenge the murder of her husband. The letter was so affecting that, when it was read in the king's council, it moved all the members to tears.

Many of the citizens of Paris, weary of the miseries of civil war, were now disposed to rally around their lawful monarch as the only mode of averting the horrible calamities which overwhelmed France. The Duke of Mayenne rigorously arrested all who were suspected of such designs, and four of the most prominent of the citizens were condemned to death. Henry immediately sent a message to the duke, that if the sentence were carried into effect, he would retaliate by putting to death some of the Catholic nobles whom he had in his power. Mayenne defiantly executed two Royalists. Henry immediately suspended upon a gibbet two unfortunate Leaguers who were his captives. This decisive reprisal accomplished its purpose, and compelled Mayenne to be more merciful.

With great energy, Henry now advanced to Tours, about one hundred and twenty miles south of Paris, on the banks of the Loire, taking every town by the way, and sweeping all opposition before him. He seldom slept more than three hours at a time, and seized his meals where he could.

"It takes Mayenne," said Henry, proudly, "more time to put on his boots than it does me to win a battle."

"Henry," remarked Pope Sextus V., sadly, "will surely, in the end, gain the day, for he spends less hours in bed than Mayenne spends at the table."

Though the armies of the League were still superior to the Royalist army, victory every where followed the banner of the king. Every day there was more and more of union and harmony in his ranks, and more and more of discord in the armies of the League. There were various aspirants for the throne in case Henry IV. could be driven from the kingdom, and all these aspirants had their partisans. The more reasonable portion of the Catholic party soon saw that there could be no end to civil war unless the rights of Henry IV. were maintained. Each day consequently witnessed accessions of powerful nobles to his side. The great mass of the people also, notwithstanding their hatred of Protestantism and devotion to the Catholic Church, found it difficult to break away from their homage to the ancient law of succession.

It was now manifest to all, that if Henry would but proclaim himself a Catholic, the war would almost instantly terminate, and the people, with almost entire unanimity, would rally around him. Henry IV. was a lawful monarch endeavoring to put down insurrection. Mayenne was a rebel contending against his king. The Pope was so unwilling to see a Protestant sovereign enthroned in France, that he issued a bull of excommunication against all who should advocate the cause of Henry IV. Many of the Royalist Catholics, however, instead of yielding to these thunders of the Vatican, sent a humble apology to the Pope for their adherence to the king, and still sustained his cause.

Henry now moved on with the strides of a conqueror, and city after city fell into his hands. Wherever he entered a city, the ever vacillating multitude welcomed him with acclamations. Regardless of the storms of winter, Henry dragged his heavy artillery through the mire and over the frozen ruts, and before the close of the year 1589 his banner waved over fifteen fortified cities and over very many minor towns. The forces of the League were entirely swept from three of the provinces of France.

Still Paris was in the hands of the Duke of Mayenne, and a large part of the kingdom was yet held in subjection by the forces of the League.

At one time, in the face of a fierce cannonade, Henry mounted the tower of a church at Meulun to ascertain the position of the enemy. As he was ascending, cannon ball passed between his legs. In returning, the stairs were found so shot away that he was compelled to let himself down by a rope. All the winter long, the storm of battle raged in every part of France, and among all the millions of the ill-fated realm, there could not then, perhaps, have been found one single prosperous and happy home.

CHAPTER X

WAR AND WOE

1590-1591

Ferocity of the combatants.--Liberality of Henry.--Preparations for a battle.--Striking phenomenon.--The omen.--Manoeuvres.--Night before the battle.--Morning of the battle.--Henry's address to his army.--The prayer of Henry.--Anecdote.--Magnanimity of Henry.--The battle of Ivry.--Heroism of Henry.--The Leaguers vanquished.--Flight of the Leaguers.--Detestable conduct of Mayenne.--Lines on the battle of Ivry.--Paris in consternation.--Inexplicable delay.--Magnanimity to the Swiss Catholics.--Paris blockaded.--Death of the Cardinal of Bourbon.--Horrors of famine.--Kindness of Henry.--Murmurs in Paris.--The assault.--The suburbs taken.--The Duchess of Montpensier.--Great clemency of Henry.--Murmurs in the camp.--Desultory warfare.--Awful condition of France.--Attempts to conciliate the Catholics.--Curious challenge.--A new dynasty contemplated.--Trouble in the camp of Henry.--Motives for abjuring Protestantism.

Civil war seems peculiarly to arouse the ferocity of man. Family quarrels are notoriously implacable. Throughout the whole kingdom of France the war raged with intense violence, brother against brother, and father against child. Farm-houses, cities, villages, were burned mercilessly. Old men, women, and children were tortured and slain with insults and derision. Maiden modesty was cruelly violated, and every species of inhumanity was practiced by the infuriated antagonists. The Catholic priests were in general conspicuous for their brutality. They resolved that the Protestant heresy should be drowned in blood and terror.

Henry IV. was peculiarly a humane man. He cherished kind feelings for all his subjects, and was perfectly willing that the Catholic religion should retain its unquestioned supremacy. His pride, however, revolted from yielding to compulsory conversion, and he also refused to become the persecutor of his former friends. Indeed, it seems probable that he was strongly inclined toward the Catholic faith as, on the whole, the safest and the best. He consequently did every thing in his power to mitigate the mercilessness of the strife, and to win his Catholic subjects by the most signal clemency. But no efforts of his could restrain his partisans in different parts of the kingdom from severe retaliation.

Through the long months of a cold and dreary winter the awful carnage continued, with success so equally balanced that there was no prospect of any termination to this most awful of national calamities. Early in March, 1590, the armies of Henry IV. and of the Duke of Mayenne began to congregate in the vicinity of Ivry, about fifty miles west of Paris, for a decisive battle. The snows of winter had nearly disappeared, and the cold rains of spring deluged the roads. The Sabbath of the eleventh of March was wet and tempestuous. As night darkened over the bleak and soaked plains of Ivry, innumerable battalions of armed men, with spears, and banners, and heavy pieces of artillery, dragged axle-deep through the mire, were dimly discerned taking positions for an approaching battle. As the blackness of midnight enveloped them, the storm increased to fearful fury. The gale fiercely swept the plain, in its loud wailings and its roar drowning every human sound. The rain, all the night long, poured down in torrents. But through the darkness and the storm, and breasting the gale, the contending hosts, without even a watch-fire to cheer the gloom, waited anxiously for the morning.

In the blackest hour of the night, a phenomenon, quite unusual at that season of the year, presented itself. The lightning gleamed in dazzling brilliance from cloud to cloud, and the thunder rolled over their heads as if an aerial army were meeting and charging in the sanguinary fight. It was an age of superstition, and the shivering soldiers thought that they could distinctly discern the banners of the battling hosts. Eagerly and with awe they watched the surgings of the strife as spirit squadrons swept to and fro with streaming banners of fire, and hurling upon each other the thunderbolts of the skies. At length the storm of battle seemed to lull, or, rather, to pass away in the distance. There was the retreat of the vanquished, the pursuit of the victors. The flash of the guns became more faint, and the roar of the artillery diminished as farther and still farther the embattled hosts vanished among the clouds. Again there was the silence of midnight, and no sounds were heard but the plashing of the rain.

The Royalists and the insurgents, each party inflamed more or less by religious fanaticism, were each disposed to regard the ethereal battle as waged between the spirits of light and the spirits of darkness, angels against fiends. Each party, of course, imagined itself as represented by the angel bands, which doubtless conquered. The phenomenon was thus, to both, the omen of success, and inspired both with new energies.

The morning dawned gloomily. Both armies were exhausted and nearly frozen by the chill storm of the night. Neither of the parties were eager to commence the fight, as each was anxious to wait for re-enforcements, which were hurrying forward, from distant posts, with the utmost possible speed. The two next days were passed in various manoeuvres to gain posts of advantage. The night of the 13th came. Henry took but two hours of repose upon a mattress, and then, every thing being arranged according to his wishes, spent nearly all the rest of the night in prayer. He urged the Catholics and the Protestants in his army to do the same, each according to the rites of his own Church. The Catholic priests and the Protestant clergy led the devotions of their respective bands, and there can be no doubt whatever that they implored the aid of God with as perfect a conviction of the righteousness of their cause as the human heart can feel.

And how was it in the army of the Duke of Mayenne? They also looked to God for support. The Pope, Christ's vicar upon earth, had blessed their banners. He had called upon all of the faithful to advocate their cause. He had anathematized their foes as the enemies of God and man, justly doomed to utter extermination. Can it be doubted that the ecclesiastics and the soldiers who surrounded the Duke of Mayenne, ready to lay down their lives for the Church, were also, many of them, sincere in their supplications? Such is bewildered, benighted man. When will he imbibe the spirit of a noble toleration--of a kind brotherhood?

The morning of the 14th of March arrived. The stars shone brilliantly in the clear, cold sky. The vast plain of Ivry and its surrounding hills gleamed with the camp-fires of the two armies, now face to face. It is impossible to estimate with precision the two forces. It is generally stated that Henry IV. had from ten to twelve thousand men, and the Duke of Mayenne from sixteen to twenty thousand.

Before the first glimmer of day, Henry mounted his horse, a powerful bay charger, and riding slowly along his lines, addressed to every company words of encouragement and hope. His spirit was subdued and his voice was softened by the influence of prayer. He attempted no lofty harangue; he gave utterance to no clarion notes of enthusiasm; but mildly, gently, with a trembling voice and often with a moistened eye, implored them to be true to God, to France, and to themselves.

"Your future fame and your personal safety," said he, "depend upon your heroism this day. The crown of France awaits the decision of your swords. If we are defeated to-day, we are defeated hopelessly, for we have no reserves upon which we can fall back."

KARTINDO PUBLISHING HOUSE (Kartindo.Com)

Then assembling nearly all his little band in a square around him, he placed himself upon an eminence where he could be seen by all, and where nearly all could hear him, and then, with clasped hands and eyes raised to Heaven, offered the following prayer--a truly extraordinary prayer, so humble and so Christian in its spirit of resignation:

"O God, I pray thee, who alone knowest the intentions of man's heart, to do thy will upon me as thou shalt judge necessary for the weal of Christendom. And wilt thou preserve me as long as thou seest it to be needful for the happiness and the repose of France, and no longer. If thou dost see that I should be one of those kings on whom thou dost lay thy wrath, take my life with my crown, and let my blood be the last poured out in this quarrel."

Then turning to his troops, he said,

"Companions, God is with us. You are to meet His enemies and ours. If, in the turmoil of the battle, you lose sight of your banner, follow the white plume upon my casque. You will find it in the road to victory and honor."

But a few hours before this, General Schomberg, who was in command of the auxiliaries furnished to Henry by Germany, urged by the importunity of his troops, ventured to ask for their pay, which was in arrears. Henry, irritated, replied,

"A man of courage would not ask for money on the eve of a battle."

The words had no sooner escaped his lips than he regretted them. Henry now rode to the quarters of this veteran officer, and thus magnanimously addressed him:

"General Schomberg, I have insulted you. As this day may be the last of my life, I would not carry away the honor of a gentleman and be unable to restore it. I know your valor, and I ask your pardon. I beseech you to forgive me and embrace me."

This was true magnanimity. General Schomberg nobly replied,

"Sire, you did, indeed, wound me yesterday, but to-day you kill me. The honor you have done me will lead me to lay down my life in your service."

KARTINDO PUBLISHING HOUSE (Kartindo.Com)

A terrible battle immediately ensued. All fought bravely, ferociously, infernally. Love and peace are the elements of heaven. Hatred and war are the elements of hell. Man, upon the battle-field, even in a good cause, must call to his aid the energies of the world of woe. Rushing squadrons swept the field, crushing beneath iron hoofs the dying and the dead. Grapeshot mowed down the crowded ranks, splintering bones, and lacerating nerves, and extorting shrieks of agony which even the thunders of the battle could not drown. Henry plunged into the thickest of the fight, every where exposing himself to peril like the humblest soldier. The conflict was too desperate to be lasting. In less than an hour the field of battle was crimson with blood and covered with mangled corpses.

The Leaguers began to waver. They broke and fled in awful confusion. The miserable fugitives were pursued and cut down by the keen swords of the cavalry, while from every eminence the cannon of the victors plowed their retreating ranks with balls. Henry himself headed the cavalry in the impetuous pursuit, that the day might be the more decisive. When he returned, covered with blood, he was greeted from his triumphant ranks with the shout, *Vive le roi!*

Marshal Biron, with a powerful reserve, had remained watching the progress of the fight, ready to avail himself of any opportunity which might present to promote or to increase the discomfiture of the foe. He now joined the monarch, saying,

"This day, sire, you have performed the part of Marshal Biron, and Marshal Biron that of the king."

"Let us praise God, marshal," answered Henry, "for the victory is his."

The routed army fled with the utmost precipitation in two directions, one division toward Chartres and the other toward Ivry. The whole Royalist army hung upon their rear, assailing them with every available missile of destruction. The Duke of Mayenne fled across the Eure. Thousands of his broken bands were crowding the shore, striving to force their way across the thronged bridge, when the Royalist cavalry, led by the monarch himself, was seen in the distance spurring furiously over the hills. Mayenne himself having passed, in order to secure his own safety, cruelly gave the command to destroy the bridge, leaving the unhappy men who had not yet crossed at the mercy of the victors. The bridge was immediately blown up. Many of those thus abandoned, in their terror cast themselves into the flooded stream, where multitudes were drowned. Others shot their horses and built a rampart of their bodies. Behind this revolting breastwork they defended themselves, until, one after another, they all fell beneath the sabres and the bullets of the Protestants. In this dreadful retreat more than two thousand were put to the sword, large numbers were drowned, and many were taken captive.

In this day, so glorious to the Royalist cause, more than one half of the army of the Leaguers were either slain or taken prisoners. Though the Duke of Mayenne escaped, many of his best generals perished upon the field of battle or were captured. It is reported that Henry shouted to his victorious troops as they were cutting down the fugitives, "Spare the French; they are our brethren."

This celebrated battle has often been the theme of the poet. But no one has done the subject better justice than Mr. Macaulay in the following spirited lines. They are intended to express the feelings of a Huguenot soldier.

THE BATTLE OF IVRY.

"The king has come to marshal us, all in his armor dressed. And he has bound a snow-white plume upon his gallant crest. He looked upon his people, and a tear was in his eye; He looked upon the traitors, and his glance was stern and high. Right graciously he smiled on us, as rolled from wing to wing, Down all our line, a deafening shout, 'God save our lord the king!' 'And if my standard-bearer fall, as fall full well he may, For never saw I promise yet of such a bloody fray, Press where ye see my white plume shine, amid the ranks of war, And be your oriflamme to-day the helmet of Navarre.'

"'Hurrah! the foes are coming! Hark to the mingled din Of fife and steed, and trump and drum, and roaring culverin! The fiery duke is pricking fast across St. Andre's plain, With all the hireling chivalry of Guelders and Almagne. Now, by the lips of those we love, fair gentlemen of France, Charge for the golden lilies now--upon them with the lance!' A thousand spurs are striking deep, a thousand spears in rest, A thousand knights are pressing close behind the snow-white crest. And on they burst, and on they rushed, while, like a guiding star, Amid the thickest carnage blazed the helmet of Navarre.

"Now, God be praised, the day is ours! Mayenne hath turned his rein, D'Aumale hath cried for quarter, the Flemish count is slain; Their ranks are breaking like thin clouds before a Biscay gale; The field is heaped with bleeding steeds, and flags, and cloven mail. And then we thought on vengeance, and all along our van, 'Remember St. Bartholomew,' was passed from man to man; But out spake gentle Henry, 'No Frenchman is my foe; Down--down with every foreigner! but let your brethren go.' Oh, was there ever such a knight, in friendship or in war, As our sovereign lord King Henry, the soldier of Navarre?"

This decisive battle established Henry on the throne. Mayenne still held Paris, and many other important fortresses in other parts of France; but his main army was defeated and dispersed, and he could no longer venture to encounter Henry in the open field. Having thrown some additional forces into Paris, which city he knew that Henry would immediately besiege, he fled to Flanders to obtain re-enforcements.

Paris was in consternation. Not a town in its vicinity could resist the conqueror. Henry was but two days' march from his rebellious capital. The Leaguers could hope for no aid for many weeks. The Royalist cause had many friends among the Parisians, eager for an opportunity to raise within their walls the banner of their lawful sovereign.

Henry had now the entire command of the Seine from Rouen to Paris. Had he immediately marched upon the capital, there can be no doubt that it would have been compelled to surrender; but, for some reason which has never been satisfactorily explained, he remained for a fortnight within one day's march of the field of Ivry. Various causes have been surmised for this unaccountable delay, but there is no authentic statement to be found in any letters written by Henry, or in any contemporaneous records. The time, however, thus lost, whatever might have been the cause, proved to him a terrible calamity. The partisans of the League in the city had time to recover from their panic, to strengthen their defenses, and to collect supplies.

One act of magnanimity which Henry performed during this interval is worthy of record. Two regiments of Swiss Catholics, who had been sent to fight beneath the banners of Mayenne, had surrendered to the royal forces. They were for a few days intensely anxious respecting their fate. Henry restored to them their ensigns, furnished them with money, supplied them with provisions, and sent them back to their native country. He gave them a letter to the Swiss cantons, with dignity reproaching them for their violation of the friendly treaty existing between Switzerland and the crown of France.

It was not until the 28th of March that Henry appeared before the walls of Paris. By this time the Leaguers had made preparations to resist him. Provisions and military stores had been accumulated. Troops had been hurried into the city, and arrangements were made to hold out till Mayenne could bring them succor. Now a siege was necessary, with all its accompaniments of blood and woe. There were now fifty thousand fighting men in the city when Henry commenced the siege with but twelve thousand foot and three thousand horse.

In this emergence the energy of Henry returned. He took possession of the river above and below the city. Batteries were reared upon the heights of Montmartre and Montfauçon, and cannon balls, portentous of the rising storm, began to fall in the thronged streets of the metropolis. In the midst of this state of things the old Cardinal of Bourbon died. The Leaguers had pronounced him king under the title of Charles X. The insurgents, discomfited in battle, and with many rival candidates ambitious of the crown, were not in a condition to attempt to elect another monarch. They thought it more prudent to combine and fight for victory, postponing until some future day their choice of a king. The Catholic priests were almost universally on their side, and urged them, by all the most sacred importunities of religion, rather to die than to allow a heretic to ascend the throne of France.

Day after day the siege continued. There were bombardments, and conflagrations, and sallies, and midnight assaults, and all the tumult, and carnage, and woe of horrid war. Three hundred thousand men, women, and children were in the beleaguered city. All supplies were cut off. Famine commenced its ravages. The wheat became exhausted, and they ate bran. The bran was all consumed, and the haggard citizens devoured the dogs and the cats. Starvation came. On parlor floors and on the hard pavement emaciate forms were stretched in the convulsions of death. The shrieks of women and children in their dying agonies fell in tones horrible to hear upon the ears of the besiegers.

The tender heart of Henry was so moved by the sufferings which he was unwillingly instrumental in inflicting, that he allowed some provisions to be carried into the city, though he thus protracted the siege. He hoped that this humanity would prove to his foes that he did not seek revenge. The Duke of Nemours, who conducted the defense, encouraged by this unmilitary humanity, that he might relieve himself from the encumbrance of useless mouths, drove several thousands out of the city. Henry, with extraordinary clemency, allowed three thousand to pass through the ranks of his army. He nobly said, "I can not bear to think of their sufferings. I had rather conquer my foes by kindness than by arms." But the number still increasing, and the inevitable effect being only to enable the combatants to hold out more stubbornly, Henry reluctantly ordered the soldiers to allow no more to pass.

The misery which now desolated the city was awful. Famine bred pestilence. Woe and death were every where. The Duke of Nemours, younger brother of the Duke of Mayenne, hoping that Mayenne might yet bring relief, still continued the defense. The citizens, tortured by the unearthly woes which pressed them on every side, began to murmur. Nemours erected scaffolds, and ordered every murmurer to be promptly hung as a partisan of Henry. Even this harsh remedy could not entirely silence fathers whose wives and children were dying of starvation before their eyes.

The Duke of Mayenne was preparing to march to the relief of the city with an army of Spaniards. Henry resolved to make an attempt to take the city by assault before their arrival. The hour was fixed at midnight, on the 24th of July. Henry watched the sublime and terrific spectacle from an observatory reared on the heights of Montmartre. In ten massive columns the Royalists made the fierce onset. The besieged were ready for them, with artillery loaded to the muzzle and with lighted torches. An eye-witness thus describes the spectacle:

"The immense city seemed instantly to blaze with conflagrations, or rather by an infinity of mines sprung in its heart. Thick whirlwinds of smoke, pierced at intervals by flashes and long lines of flame, covered the doomed city. The blackness of darkness at one moment enveloped it. Again it blazed forth as if it were a sea of fire. The roar of cannon, the clash of arms, and the shouts of the combatants added to the horrors of the night."

By this attack all of the suburbs were taken, and the condition of the besieged rendered more hopeless and miserable. There is no siege upon record more replete with horrors. The flesh of the dead was eaten. The dry bones of the cemetery were ground up for bread. Starving mothers ate their children. It is reported that the Duchess of Montpensier was offered three thousand crowns for her dog. She declined the offer, saying that she should keep it to eat herself as her last resource.

The compassion of Henry triumphed again and again over his military firmness. He allowed the women and children to leave the city, then the ecclesiastics, then the starving poor, then the starving rich. Each of these acts of generosity added to the strength of his foes. The famished Leaguers were now in a condition to make but a feeble resistance. Henry was urged to take the city by storm. He could easily do this, but fearful slaughter would be the inevitable result. For this reason Henry refused, saying,

"I am their father and their king. I can not hear the recital of their woes without the deepest sympathy. I would gladly relieve them. I can not prevent those who are possessed with the fury of the League from perishing, but to those who seek my clemency I must open my arms."

Early in August, more than thirty thousand within the walls of the city had perished by famine. Mayenne now marched to the relief of Paris. Henry, unwisely, military critics say, raised the siege and advanced to meet him, hoping to compel him to a decisive battle. Mayenne skillfully avoided a battle, and still more skillfully threw abundant supplies into the city.

And now loud murmurs began to arise in the camp of Henry. Many of the most influential of the Catholics who adhered to his cause, disheartened by this result and by the indications of an endless war, declared that it was in vain to hope that any Protestant could be accepted as King of France. The soldiers could not conceal their discouragement, and the cause of the king was involved anew in gloom.

Still Henry firmly kept the field, and a long series of conflicts ensued between detachments of the Royalist army and portions of the Spanish troops under the command of the Duke of Mayenne and the Duke of Parma. The energy of the king was roused to the utmost. Victory accompanied his marches, and his foes were driven before him.

The winter of 1591 had now arrived, and still unhappy France was one wide and wasted battle-field. Confusion, anarchy, and misery every where reigned. Every village had its hostile partisans. Catholic cities were besieged by Protestants, and Protestant towns by Catholics. In the midst of these terrible scenes, Henry had caught a glimpse, at the chateau of Coeuvres, of the beautiful face of Gabrielle d'Estrées. Ignobly yielding to a guilty passion, he again forgot the great affairs of state and the woes of his distracted country in the pursuit of this new amour. The history of this period contains but a monotonous record of the siege of innumerable towns, with all the melancholy accompaniments of famine and blood. Summer came and went, and hardly a sound of joy was heard amid all the hills and valleys of beautiful but war-scathed France.

KARTINDO PUBLISHING HOUSE (Kartindo.Com)

There was great division existing among the partisans of the League, there being several candidates for the throne. There was but one cause of division in the ranks of Henry. That he was the legitimate sovereign all admitted. It was evident to all that, would Henry but abjure Protestantism and embrace the Catholic faith, nearly all opposition to him would instantly cease. Many pamphlets were issued by the priests urging the iniquity of sustaining a *heretic* upon the throne. The Pope had not only anathematized the heretical sovereign, but had condemned to eternal flames all who should maintain his cause.

Henry had no objection to Catholicism. It was the religion of five sixths of his subjects. He was now anxious to give his adherence to that faith, could he contrive some way to do it with decency. He issued many decrees to conciliate the Romanists. He proclaimed that he had never yet had time to examine the subject of religious faith; that he was anxious for instruction; that he was ready to submit to the decision of a council; and that under no circumstances would he suffer any change in France detrimental to the Catholic religion. At the same time, with energy which reflects credit upon his name, he declared the bull fulminated against him by Gregory XIV. as abusive, seditious, and damnable, and ordered it to be burned by the public hangman.

By the middle of November, 1591, Henry, with an army of thirty-five thousand men, surrounded the city of Rouen. Queen Elizabeth had again sent him aid. The Earl of Essex joined the royal army with a retinue whose splendor amazed the impoverished nobles of France. His own gorgeous dress, and the caparisons of his steed, were estimated to be worth sixty thousand crowns of gold. The garrison of Rouen was under the command of Governor Villars. Essex sent a curious challenge to Villars, that if he would meet him on horseback or on foot, in armor or doublet, he would maintain against him man to man, twenty to twenty, or sixty to sixty. To this defiance the earl added, "I am thus ready to prove that the cause of the king is better than that of the League, that Essex is a braver man than Villars, and that my mistress is more beautiful than yours." Villars declined the challenge, declaring, however, that the three assertions were false, but that he did not trouble himself much about the respective beauty of their mistresses.

The weary siege continued many weeks, varied with fierce sallies and bloody skirmishes. Henry labored in the trenches like a common soldier, and shared every peril. He was not wise in so doing, for his life was of far too much value to France to be thus needlessly periled.

The influential Leaguers in Paris now formed the plan to found a new dynasty in France by uniting in marriage the young Duke of Guise--son of Henry of Guise who had been assassinated--with Isabella, the daughter of Philip II., King of Spain. This secured for their cause all the energies of the Spanish monarchy. This plan immediately introduced serious discord between Mayenne and his Spanish allies, as Mayenne hoped for the crown for himself. About the same time Pope Gregory XIV. died, still more depressing the prospects of Mayenne; but, with indomitable vigor of intrigue and of battle, he still continued to guide the movements of the League, and to watch for opportunities to secure for himself the crown of France.

The politics of the nation were now in an inextricable labyrinth of confusion. Henry IV. was still sustained by the Protestants, though they were ever complaining that he favored too much the Catholics. He was also sustained by a portion of the moderate Catholics. They were, however, quite lukewarm in their zeal, and were importunately demanding that he should renounce the Protestant faith and avow himself a Catholic, or they would entirely abandon him. The Swiss and Germans in his ranks were filling the camp with murmurs, demanding their arrears of pay. The English troops furnished him by Elizabeth refused to march from the coast to penetrate the interior.

The League was split into innumerable factions, some in favor of Mayenne, others supporting the young Cardinal of Bourbon, and others still advocating the claims of the young Duke of Guise and the Infanta of Spain. They were all, however, united by a common detestation of Protestantism and an undying devotion to the Church of Rome.

In the mean time, though the siege of Rouen was pressed with great vigor, all efforts to take the place were unavailing. Henry was repeatedly baffled and discomfited, and it became daily more evident that, as a Protestant, he never could occupy a peaceful throne in Catholic France. Even many of the Protestant leaders, who were politicians rather than theologians, urged Henry to become a Catholic, as the only possible means of putting an end to this cruel civil war. They urged that while his adoption of the Catholic faith would reconcile the Catholics, the Protestants, confiding in the freedom of faith and worship which his just judgment would secure to them, would prefer him for their sovereign to any other whom they could hope to obtain. Thus peace would be restored to distracted France. Henry listened with a willing mind to these suggestions. To give assurance to the Catholics of his sincerity, he sent embassadors to Rome to treat with the Pope in regard to his reconciliation with the Church.

KARTINDO PUBLISHING HOUSE (Kartindo.Com)

CHAPTER XI

THE CONVERSION OF THE KING

1593-1595

Advice of the Duke of Sully.--Perplexity of Henry.--Theological argument of Sully.--Philip of Mornay, Lord of Plessis.--Inflexible integrity of Mornay.--Mornay's reply to Henry III.--Attempt to bribe Mornay.--His address to the courtiers.--Indecision of Henry.--Process of conversion.--Testimony of Sully.--Gabrielle d'Estrées.--Influence of Gabrielle.--Abjuration of Protestantism.--Public adoption of the Catholic faith.--Ceremony in the Church of St. Denis.--Alleged sincerity of the king.--Other motives assigned.--Political effects of Henry's conversion.--Satisfaction of the people.--Ferocity of the Pope.--Coronation of the king.--Paris secretly surrendered.--The entry to Paris.--Noble conduct.--Justice of Henry IV.--Joy in Paris.--Reconciliation with the Pope.--Henry chastised by proxy.--The farce.--Cause of the war.--The Protestants still persecuted.--Scene of massacre.--Dissatisfaction of both Catholics and Protestants.--Complaints of the Reformed Churches of France.

This bloody war of the succession had now desolated France for four years. The Duke of Sully, one of the most conspicuous of the political Calvinists, was at last induced to give his influence to lead the king to accept the Catholic faith. Sully had been Henry's companion from childhood. Though not a man of deep religious convictions, he was one of the most illustrious of men in ability, courage, and integrity. Conversing with Henry upon the distracted affairs of state, he said, one day,

"That you should wait for me, being a Protestant, to counsel you to go to mass, is a thing you should not do, although I will boldly declare to you that it is the prompt and easy way of destroying all malign projects. You will thus meet no more enemies, sorrows, nor difficulties *in this world*. As to the *other world*," he continued, smiling, "I can not answer for that."

The king continued in great perplexity. He felt that it was degrading to change his religion upon apparent compulsion, or for the accomplishment of any selfish purpose. He knew that he must expose himself to the charge of apostasy and of hypocrisy in affirming a change of belief, even to accomplish so

KARTINDO PUBLISHING HOUSE (Kartindo.Com)

meritorious a purpose as to rescue a whole nation from misery. These embarrassments to a vacillating mind were terrible.

Early one morning, before rising, he sent for Sully. The duke found the king sitting up in his bed, "scratching his head in great perplexity." The political considerations in favor of the change urged by the duke could not satisfy fully the mind of the king. He had still some conscientious scruples, imbibed from the teachings of a pious and sainted mother. The illustrious warrior, financier, and diplomatist now essayed the availability of theological considerations, and urged the following argument of Jesuitical shrewdness:

"I hold it certain," argued the duke, "that whatever be the exterior form of the religion which men profess, if they live in the observation of the Decalogue, believe in the Creed of the apostles, love God with all their heart, have charity toward their neighbor, hope in the mercy of God, and to obtain salvation by the death, merits, and justice of Jesus Christ, they can not fail to be saved."

Henry caught eagerly at this plausible argument. The Catholics say that no Protestant can be saved, but the Protestants admit that a Catholic may be, if in heart honest, just, and true. The sophistry of the plea in behalf of an *insincere* renunciation of faith is too palpable to influence any mind but one eager to be convinced. The king was counseled to obey the Decalogue, which *forbids false witness*, while at the same time he was to be guilty of an act of fraud and hypocrisy.

But Henry had another counselor. Philip of Mornay, Lord of Plessis, had imbibed from his mother's lips a knowledge of the religion of Jesus Christ. His soul was endowed by nature with the most noble lineaments, and he was, if man can judge, a devoted and exalted Christian. There was no one, in those stormy times, more illustrious as a warrior, statesman, theologian, and orator. "We can not," says a French writer, "indicate a species of merit in which he did not excel, except that he did not advance his own fortune." When but twelve years of age, a priest exhorted him to beware of the opinions of the Protestants.

"I am resolved," Philip replied, firmly, "to remain steadfast in what I have learned of the service of God. When I doubt any point, I will diligently examine the Gospels and the Acts of the Apostles."

His uncle, the Archbishop of Rheims, advised him to read the fathers of the Church, and promised him the revenues of a rich abbey and the prospect of still higher advancement if he would adhere to the Catholic religion. Philip read the fathers and declined the bribe, saying,

"I must trust to God for what I need."

Almost by a miracle he had escaped the Massacre of St. Bartholomew and fled to England. The Duke of Anjou, who had become King of Poland, wishing to conciliate the Protestants, wrote to Mornay in his poverty and exile, proposing to him a place in his ministry. The noble man replied,

"I will never enter the service of those who have shed the blood of my brethren."

He soon joined the feeble court of the King of Navarre, and adhered conscientiously, through all vicissitudes, to the Protestant cause. Henry IV. was abundantly capable of appreciating such a character, and he revered and loved Mornay. His services were invaluable to Henry, for he seemed to be equally skillful in nearly all departments of knowledge and of business. He could with equal facility guide an army, construct a fortress, and write a theological treatise. Many of the most important state papers of Henry IV. he hurriedly wrote upon the field of battle or beneath his wind-shaken tent. Henry III., on one occasion, had said to him,

"How can a man of your intelligence and ability be a Protestant? Have you never read the Catholic doctors?"

"Not only have I read the Catholic doctors," Mornay replied, "but I have read them with eagerness; for I am flesh and blood like other men, and I was not born without ambition. I should have been very glad to find something to flatter my conscience that I might participate in the favors and honors you distribute, and from which my religion excludes me; but, above all, I find something which fortifies my faith, and the world must yield to conscience."

The firm Christian principles of Philip of Mornay were now almost the only barrier which stood in the way of the conversion of Henry. The Catholic lords offered Mornay twenty thousand crowns of gold if he would no more awaken the scruples of the king. Nobly he replied,

"The conscience of my master is not for sale, neither is mine."

Great efforts were then made to alienate Henry from his faithful minister. Mornay by chance one day entered the cabinet of the king, where his enemies were busy in their cabals. In the boldness of an integrity which never gave him cause to blush, he thus addressed them in the presence of the sovereign:

"It is hard, gentlemen, to prevent the king my master from speaking to his faithful servant. The proposals which I offer the king are such that I can pronounce them distinctly before you all. I propose to him to serve God with a good conscience; to keep Him in view in every action; to quiet the schism which is in his state by a holy reformation of the Church, and to be an example for all Christendom during all time to come. Are these things to be spoken in a corner? Do you wish me to counsel him to go to mass? With what conscience shall I advise if I do not first go myself? And what is religion, if it can be laid aside like a shirt?"

The Catholic nobles felt the power of this moral courage and integrity, and one of them, Marshal d'Aumont, yielding to a generous impulse, exclaimed,

"You are better than we are, Monsieur Mornay; and if I said, two days ago, that it was necessary to give you a pistol-shot in the head, I say to-day entirely the contrary, and that you should have a statue."

Henry, however, was a politician, not a Christian; and nothing is more amazing than the deaf ear which even apparently good men can turn to the pleadings of conscience when they are involved in the mazes of political ambition. The process of conversion was, for decency's sake, protracted and ostentatious. As Henry probably had no fixed religious principles, he could with perhaps as much truth say that he was a Catholic as that he was a Protestant.

On the 23d of July the king listened to a public argument, five hours in length, from the Archbishop of Bourges, upon the points of essential difference between the two antagonistic creeds. Henry found the reasoning of the archbishop most comfortably persuasive, and, having separated himself for a time from Mornay, he professed to be solemnly convinced that the Roman Catholic faith was the true religion. Those who knew Henry the best declare that he was sincere in the change, and his subsequent life seems certainly to indicate that he was so. The Duke of Sully, who refused to follow Henry into the Catholic Church, records,

"As uprightness and sincerity formed the depth of his heart, as they did of his

KARTINDO PUBLISHING HOUSE (Kartindo.Com)

words, I am persuaded that nothing would have been capable of making him embrace a religion which he internally despised, or of which he even doubted."

In view of this long interview with the Archbishop of Bourges, Henry wrote to the frail but beautiful Gabrielle d'Estrées,

"I began this morning to speak to the bishops. On Sunday I shall take the perilous leap." The king's connection with Gabrielle presented another strong motive to influence his conversion. Henry, when a mere boy, had been constrained by political considerations to marry the worthless and hateful sister of Charles IX. For the wife thus coldly received he never felt an emotion of affection. She was an unblushing profligate. The king, in one of his campaigns, met the beautiful maiden Gabrielle in the chateau of her father. They both immediately loved each other, and a relation prohibited by the divine law soon existed between them. Never, perhaps, was there a better excuse for unlawful love. But guilt ever brings woe. Neither party were happy. Gabrielle felt condemned and degraded, and urged the king to obtain a divorce from the notoriously profligate Marguerite of Valois, that their union might be sanctioned by the rites of religion. Henry loved Gabrielle tenderly. Her society was his chiefest joy, and it is said that he ever remained faithful to her. He was anxious for a divorce from Marguerite, and for marriage with Gabrielle. But this divorce could only be obtained through the Pope. Hence Gabrielle exerted all her influence to lead the king into the Church, that this most desired end might be attained.

The king now openly proclaimed his readiness to renounce Protestantism and to accept the Papal Creed. The Catholic bishops prepared an act of abjuration, rejecting, very decisively, one after another, every distinguishing article of the Protestant faith. The king glanced his eye over it, and instinctively recoiled from an act which he seemed to deem humiliating. He would only consent to sign a very brief declaration, in six lines, of his return to the Church of Rome. The paper, however, which he had rejected, containing the emphatic recantation of every article of the Protestant faith, was sent to the Pope with the forged signature of the king.

The final act of renunciation was public, and was attended with much dramatic pomp, in the great church of St. Denis. It was Sunday, the twenty-fifth of July, 1593. The immense cathedral was richly decorated. Flowers were scattered upon the pavements, and garlands and banners festooned the streets and the dwellings.

KARTINDO PUBLISHING HOUSE (Kartindo.Com)

At eight o'clock in the morning Henry presented himself before the massive portals of the Cathedral. He was dressed in white satin, with a black mantle and chapeau. The white plume, which both pen and pencil have rendered illustrious, waved from his hat. He was surrounded by a gorgeous retinue of nobles and officers of the crown. Several regiments of soldiers, in the richest uniform, preceded and followed him as he advanced toward the church. Though a decree had been issued strictly prohibiting the populace from being present at the ceremony, an immense concourse thronged the streets, greeting the monarch with enthusiastic cries of "*Vive le roi!*"

[Illustration: THE ACT OF ABJURING PROTESTANTISM.]

The Archbishop of Bourges was seated at the entrance of the church in a chair draped with white damask. The Cardinal of Bourbon, and several bishops glittering in pontifical robes, composed his brilliant retinue. The monks of St. Denis were also in attendance, clad in their sombre attire, bearing the cross, the Gospels, and the holy water. Thus the train of the exalted dignitary of the Church even eclipsed in splendor the suite of the king.

As Henry approached the door of the church, the archbishop, as if to repel intrusion, imperiously inquired,

"Who are you?"

"I am the king," Henry modestly replied.

"What do you desire?" demanded the archbishop.

"I ask," answered the king, "to be received into the bosom of the Catholic, Apostolic, and Roman religion."

"Do you desire this *sincerely*?" rejoined the archbishop.

"I do," the king replied. Then kneeling at the feet of the prelate, he pronounced the following oath:

"I protest and swear, in the presence of Almighty God, to live and die in the Catholic, Apostolic, and Roman religion; to protect and defend it against all its enemies at the hazard of my blood and life, renouncing all heresies contrary to it."

The king then placed a copy of this oath in writing in the hands of the archbishop, and kissed the consecrated ring upon his holy finger. Then entering the Cathedral, he received the absolution of his sins and the benediction of the Church. A *Te Deum* was then sung, high mass was solemnized, and thus the imposing ceremony was terminated.

It is easy to treat this whole affair as a farce. The elements of ridicule are abundant. But it was by no means a farce in the vast influences which it evolved. Catholic historians have almost invariably assumed that the king acted in perfect good faith, being fully convinced by the arguments of the Church. Even Henry's Protestant friend, the Duke of Sully, remarks,

"I should betray the cause of truth if I suffered it even to be suspected that policy, the threats of the Catholics, the fatigue of labor, the desire of rest, and of freeing himself from the tyranny of foreigners, or even the good of the people, had entirely influenced the king's resolution. As far as I am able to judge of the heart of this prince, which I believe I know better than any other person, it was, indeed, these considerations which first hinted to him the necessity of his conversion; but, in the end, he became convinced in his own mind that the Catholic religion was the safest."

Others have affirmed that it was a shameful act of apostasy, in which the king, stimulated by ambition and unlawful love, stooped to hypocrisy, and feigned a conversion which in heart he despised. He is represented as saying, with levity,

"Paris is well worth a mass."

Others still assert that Henry was humanely anxious to arrest the horrors of civil war; to introduce peace to distracted France, and to secure the Protestants from oppression. His acceptance of the Catholic faith was the only apparent way of accomplishing these results. Being a humane man, but not a man of established Christian principle, he deemed it his duty to pursue the course which would accomplish such results. The facts, so far as known, are before the reader, and each one can form his own judgment.

The announcement throughout the kingdom that Henry had become a Catholic almost immediately put an end to the civil war. Incited by the royal example, many of the leading Protestants, nobles and gentlemen, also renounced Protestantism, and conformed to the religion of the state. The chiefs of the League, many of whom were ambitious political partisans rather than zealous theologians, and who were clamorous for Catholicism only as the means of obtaining power, at once relinquished all hope of victory. For a time, however, they still assumed a hostile attitude, and heaped unmeasured ridicule upon what they styled the feigned conversion of the king. They wished to compel the monarch to purchase their adhesion at as dear a price as possible.

Many important cities surrendered to the royal cause under the stipulation that the preaching of the Protestants should be utterly prohibited in their precincts and suburbs. Even the Pope, Clement VIII., a weak and bigoted man, for a time refused to ratify the act of the Archbishop of Bourges in absolving Henry from the pains and penalties of excommunication. He forbade the envoy of Henry to approach the Vatican. The Duke of Nevers, who was the appointed envoy, notwithstanding this prohibition, persisted in his endeavors to obtain an audience; but the Pope was anxious to have the crown of France in the possession of one whose Catholic zeal could not be questioned. He would much have preferred to see the fanatic Duke of Mayenne upon the throne, or to have promoted the Spanish succession. He therefore treated the Duke of Nevers with great indignity, and finally gave him an abrupt dismission.

But the mass of the French people, longing for repose, gladly accepted the conversion of the king. One after another the leaders of the League gave in their adhesion to the royal cause. The Duke of Mayenne, however, held out, Paris being still in his possession, and several other important cities and fortresses being garrisoned by his troops. The Pope, at length, having vainly done every thing in his power to rouse France and Catholic Europe to resist Henry, condescended to negotiate. His spirit may be seen in the atrocious conditions which he proposed. As the price of his absolution, he required that Henry should abrogate every edict of toleration, that he should exclude Protestants from all public offices, and that he should exterminate them from the kingdom as soon as possible.

To these demands Henry promptly replied, "I should be justly accused of shamelessness and ingratitude if, after having received such signal services from the Protestants, I should thus persecute them."

Henry was fully aware of the influence of forms upon the imaginations of the people. He accordingly made preparations for his coronation. The event was celebrated with great pomp, in the city of Chartres, on the 27th of February,

1594. The Leaguers were now quite disheartened. Every day their ranks were diminishing. The Duke of Mayenne, apprehensive that his own partisans might surrender Paris to the king, and that thus he might be taken prisoner, on the 6th of March, with his wife and children, left the city, under the pretense of being called away by important business.

Three hours after midnight of the 21st of the month the gates were secretly thrown open, and a body of the king's troops entered the metropolis. They marched rapidly along the silent streets, hardly encountering the slightest opposition. Before the morning dawned they had taken possession of the bridges, the squares, and the ramparts, and their cannon were planted so as to sweep all the important streets and avenues.

The citizens, aroused by the tramp of infantry and of cavalry, and by the rumbling of the heavy artillery over the pavements, rose from their beds, and crowded the windows, and thronged the streets. In the early dawn, the king, accompanied by the officers of his staff, entered the capital. He was dressed in the garb of a civilian, and was entirely unarmed. All were ready to receive him. Shouts of "Peace! peace! Long live the king!" reverberated in tones of almost delirious joy through the thoroughfares of the metropolis. Henry thus advanced through the ranks of the rejoicing people to the great cathedral of Notre Dame, where mass was performed. He then proceeded to the royal palace of the Louvre, which his officers had already prepared for his reception. All the bells of the city rung their merriest chimes, bands of music pealed forth their most exultant strains, and the air was rent with acclamations as the king, after all these long and bloody wars, thus peacefully took possession of the capital of his kingdom.

In this hour of triumph Henry manifested the most noble clemency. He issued a decree declaring that no citizen who had been in rebellion against him should be molested. Even the Spanish troops who were in the city to fight against him were permitted to depart with their arms in their hands. As they defiled through the gate of St. Denis, the king stood by a window, and, lifting his hat, respectfully saluted the officers. They immediately approached the magnanimous monarch, and, bending the knee, thanked him feelingly for his great clemency. The king courteously replied,

"Adieu, gentlemen, adieu! Commend me to your master, and go in peace, but do not come back again."

La Noue, one of Henry's chief supporters, as he was entering the city, had his baggage attached for an old debt. Indignantly he hastened to the king to complain of the outrage. The just monarch promptly but pleasantly replied,

"We must pay our debts, La Noue. I pay mine." Then drawing his faithful servant aside, he gave him his jewels to pledge for the deliverance of his baggage. The king was so impoverished that he had not money sufficient to pay the debt.

These principles of justice and magnanimity, which were instinctive with the king, and which were daily manifested in multiplied ways, soon won to him nearly all hearts. All France had writhed in anguish through years of war and misery. Peace, the greatest of all earthly blessings, was now beginning to diffuse its joys. The happiness of the Parisians amounted almost to transport. It was difficult for the king to pass through the streets, the crowd so thronged him with their acclamations. Many other important towns soon surrendered. But the haughty Duke of Mayenne refused to accept the proffered clemency, and, strengthened by the tremendous spiritual power of the head of the Church, still endeavored to arouse the energies of Papal fanaticism in Flanders and in Spain.

Soon, however, the Pope became convinced that all further resistance would be in vain. It was but compromising his dignity to be vanquished, and he accordingly decided to accept reconciliation. In yielding to this, the Pope stooped to the following silly farce, quite characteristic of those days of darkness and delusion. It was deemed necessary that the king should do penance for his sins before he could be received to the bosom of holy mother Church. It was proper that the severe mother should chastise her wayward child. "Whom the Lord loveth he chasteneth."

It was the sixteenth of September, 1595. The two embassadors of Henry IV. kneeled upon the vestibule of one of the churches in Rome as unworthy to enter. In strains of affected penitence, they chanted the *Miserere*--"Have mercy, Lord." At the close of every verse they received, in the name of their master, the blows of a little switch on their shoulders. The king, having thus made expiation for his sins, through the reception of this chastisement by proxy, and having thus emphatically acknowledged the authority of the sacred mother, received the absolution of the vicar of Christ, and was declared to be worthy of the loyalty of the faithful.

We have called this a *farce*. And yet can it be justly called so? The proud spirit of the king must indeed have been humiliated ere he could have consented to such a degradation. The spirit ennobled can bid defiance to any amount of corporeal pain. It is ignominy alone which can punish the soul. The Pope triumphed; the monarch was flogged. It is but just to remark that the friends of Henry deny that he was accessory to this act of humiliation.

The atrocious civil war, thus virtually, for a time, terminated, was caused by the Leaguers, who had bound themselves together in a *secret society* for the persecution of the Protestants. Their demand was inexorable that the Protestants throughout France should be proscribed and exterminated. The Protestants were compelled to unite in self-defense. They only asked for liberty to worship God according to their understanding of the teachings of the Bible. Henry, to conciliate the Catholics, was now compelled to yield to many of their claims which were exceedingly intolerant. He did this very unwillingly, for it was his desire to do every thing in his power to meliorate the condition of his Protestant friends. But, notwithstanding all the kind wishes of the king, the condition of the Protestants was still very deplorable. Public opinion was vehemently against them. The magistrates were every where their foes, and the courts of justice were closed against all their appeals. Petty persecution and tumultuary violence in a thousand forms annoyed them. During the year of Henry's coronation, a Protestant congregation in Chalaigneraie was assailed by a Catholic mob instigated by the Leaguers, and two hundred men, women, and children were massacred. A little boy eight years old, in the simplicity of his heart, offered eight coppers which he had in his pocket to ransom his life; but the merciless fanatics struck him down. Most of these outrages were committed with entire impunity. The king had even felt himself forced to take the oath, "I will endeavor with all my power, in good faith, to drive from my jurisdiction and estates all the heretics denounced by the Church."

The Protestants, finding themselves thus denounced as enemies, and being cut off from all ordinary privileges and from all common justice, decided, for mutual protection, vigorously to maintain their political organization. The king, though he feigned to be displeased, still encouraged them to do so. Though the Protestants were few in numbers, they were powerful in intelligence, rank, and energy; and in their emergencies, the strong arm of England was ever generously extended for their aid. The king was glad to avail himself of their strength to moderate the intolerant demands of the Leaguers. Many of the Protestants complained bitterly that the king had abandoned them. On the other hand, the haughty leaders of the League clamored loudly that the king was not a true son of the Church, and, in multiform conspiracies, they sought his death by assassination.

The Protestants held several large assemblies in which they discussed their affairs. They drew up an important document--an address to the king, entitled, "Complaints of the Reformed Churches of France." Many pages were filled with a narrative of the intolerable grievances they endured. This paper contained, in conclusion, the following noble words:

"And yet, sire, we have among us no Jacobins or Jesuits who wish for your life, or Leaguers who aspire to your crown. We have never presented, instead of petitions, the points of our swords. We are rewarded with *considerations of state*. It is not yet time, they say, to grant us an edict. And yet, after thirty-five years of persecution, ten years of banishment by the edicts of the League, eight years of the king's reign, four years of proscription, we are still under the necessity of imploring from your majesty an edict which shall allow us to enjoy what is common to all your subjects. The sole glory of God, the liberty of our consciences, the repose of the state, the security of our property and our lives-- this is the summit of our wishes, and the end of our requests."

KARTINDO PUBLISHING HOUSE (Kartindo.Com)

CHAPTER XII

REIGN AND DEATH OF HENRY IV

1596-1610

Mayenne professes reconciliation.--Terms exacted by the duke.--Interview between Henry and the duke.--Henry's revenge.--Hostility of Spain and Flanders.--Calais taken by the Leaguers.--Movement of the nobles.--Energetic reply of the king.--Dark days.--Singular accident.--Deplorable state of France.-- Poverty of the king.--Depression of the king.--The Duke of Sully.--Siege of Amiens.--Its capitulation.--The Edict of Nantes.--Provisions of the edict.-- Clamors of the Catholics.--Toleration slowly learned.--Dissatisfaction of both parties.--Progress of affairs.--Prosperity in the kingdom.--Henry's illness.-- Devotion of his subjects.--Hostility of the nobles.--The Marchioness of Verneuil.--Integrity of Sully.--The slave of love.--The king's greatness.-- Financial skill of Sully.--Co-operation of Henry.--Solicitations of Gabrielle.-- Her death.--Grief of the king.--The divorce.--Henrietta d'Entragues.--Bold fidelity of Sully.--Marriage to Maria of Medici.--Anecdote.--Grand political scheme.--Mode of preventing religious quarrels.--Assassination of the king.-- Character of Henry IV.--The truth to be enforced.--Free speech.--Free press.-- Free men.--Practical application of the moral.

The reconciliation of the king with the Pope presented a favorable opportunity for the Duke of Mayenne, consistently with his pride, to abandon the hopeless conflict. He declared that, as the Pope had accepted the conversion of the king, all his scruples were removed, and that he could now conscientiously accept him as the sovereign of France. But the power of the haughty duke may be seen in the terms he exacted.

The king was compelled to declare, though he knew to the contrary, that, all things considered, it was evident that neither the princes nor the princesses of the League were at all implicated in the assassination of Henry III., and to stop all proceedings in Parliament in reference to that atrocious murder. Three fortified cities were surrendered to the duke, to be held by him and his partisans for six years, in pledge for the faithful observance of the terms of the capitulation. The king also assumed all the debts which Mayenne had contracted during the war, and granted a term of six weeks to all the Leaguers who were still in arms to give in their adhesion and to accept his clemency.

The king was at this time at Monceaux. The Duke of Mayenne hastened to meet him. He found Henry riding on horseback in the beautiful park of that place with the fair Gabrielle, and accompanied by the Duke of Sully. Mayenne, in compliance with the obsequious etiquette of those days, kneeled humbly before the king, embraced his knees, and, assuring him of his entire devotion for the future, thanked the monarch for having delivered him "from the arrogance of the Spaniards and from the cunning of the Italians."

Henry, who had a vein of waggery about him, immediately raised the duke, embraced him with the utmost cordiality, and, taking his arm, without any allusion whatever to their past difficulties, led him through the park, pointing out to him, with great volubility and cheerfulness, the improvements he was contemplating.

Henry was a well-built, vigorous man, and walked with great rapidity. Mayenne was excessively corpulent, and lame with the gout. With the utmost difficulty he kept up with the king, panting, limping, and his face blazing with the heat. Henry, with sly malice, for some time appeared not to notice the sufferings of his victim; then, with a concealed smile, he whispered to Sully,

"If I walk this great fat body much longer, I shall avenge myself without any further trouble." Then turning to Mayenne, he added, "Tell me the truth, cousin, do I not walk a little too fast for you?"

"Sire," exclaimed the puffing duke, "I am almost dead with fatigue."

"There's my hand," exclaimed the kind-hearted king, again cordially embracing the duke. "Take it, for, on my life, this is all the vengeance I shall ever seek."

[Illustration: THE RECONCILIATION WITH MAYENNE.]

There were still parts of the kingdom which held out against Henry, and Spain and Flanders freely supplied men and ammunition to the fragments of the League. Calais was in the hands of the enemy. Queen Elizabeth of England had ceased to take much interest in the conflict since the king had gone over to the Catholics. When Calais was besieged by the foe, before its surrender she offered to send her fleet for its protection if Henry would give the city to her.

Henry tartly replied, "I had rather be plundered by my enemies than by my friends."

The queen was offended, sent no succor, and Calais passed into the hands of the Leaguers. The king was exceedingly distressed at the loss of this important town. It indicated new and rising energy on the part of his foes. The more fanatical Catholics all over the kingdom, who had never been more than half reconciled to Henry, were encouraged to think that, after all their defeats, resistance might still be successful. The heroic energies of the king were, however, not depressed by this great disaster. When its surrender was announced, turning to the gentlemen of his court, he calmly said,

"My friends, there is no remedy. Calais is taken, but we must not lose our courage. It is in the midst of disasters that bold men grow bolder. Our enemies have had their turn. With God's blessing, who has never abandoned me when I have prayed to him with my whole heart, we shall yet have ours. At any event, I am greatly comforted by the conviction that I have omitted nothing that was possible to save the city. All of its defenders have acquitted themselves loyally and nobly. Let us not reproach them. On the contrary, let us do honor to their generous defense. And now let us rouse our energies to retake the city, that it may remain in the hands of the Spaniards not so many days as our ancestors left it years in the hands of the English."

A large body of the nobles now combined to extort from the king some of the despotic feudal privileges which existed in the twelfth century. They thought that in this hour of reverse Henry would be glad to purchase their powerful support by surrendering many of the prerogatives of the crown. After holding a meeting, they appointed the Duke of Montpensier, who was very young and self-sufficient, to present their demands to the king. Their plan was this, that the king should consent to the division of France into several large departments, over each of which, as a vassal prince, some distinguished nobleman should reign, collecting his own revenues and maintaining his own army. Each of these vassal nobles was to be bound, when required, to furnish a military contingent to their liege lord the king.

Montpensier entered the presence of the monarch, and in a long discourse urged the insulting proposal. The king listened calmly, and without interrupting him, to the end. Then, in tones unimpassioned, but firm and deliberate, he replied,

"My cousin, you must be insane. Such language coming from *you*, and addressed to *me*, leads me to think that I am in a dream. Views so full of insult to the sovereign, and ruin to the state, can not have originated in your benevolent and upright mind. Think you that the people, having stripped me of the august prerogatives of royalty, would respect in you the rights of a prince of the blood? Did I believe that you, in heart, desired to see me thus humiliated, I would teach you that such an offense is not to be committed with impunity. My cousin, abandon these follies. Reveal not your accomplices, but reply to them that you yourself have such a horror of these propositions that you will hold him as a deadly enemy who shall ever speak to you of them again."

This firmness crushed the conspiracy; but still darkness and gloom seemed to rest upon unhappy France. The year 1596 was one of famine and of pestilence. "We had," says a writer of the times, "summer in April, autumn in May, and winter in June." In the city and in the country, thousands perished of starvation. Famishing multitudes crowded to the gates of the city in search of food, but in the city the plague had broken forth. The authorities drove the mendicants back into the country. They carried with them the awful pestilence in every direction. At the same time, several attempts were made to assassinate the king. Though he escaped the knife of the assassin, he came near losing his life by a singular accident.

The Princess of Navarre, sister of the king, had accompanied him, with the rest of the court, into Picardy. She was taken suddenly ill. The king called to see her, carrying in his arms his infant son, the idolized child of the fair Gabrielle. While standing by the bedside of his sister, from some unexplained cause, the flooring gave way beneath them. Henry instinctively sprang upon the bed with his child. Providentially, that portion of the floor remained firm, while all the rest was precipitated with a crash into the rooms below. Neither Henry, his sister, or his child sustained any injury.

The financial condition of the empire was in a state of utter ruin--a ruin so hopeless that the almost inconceivable story is told that the king actually suffered both for food and raiment. He at times made himself merry with his own ragged appearance. At one time he said gayly, when the Parliament sent the president, Seguier, to remonstrate against a fiscal edict,

"I only ask to be treated as they treat the monks, with food and clothing. Now, Mr. President, I often have not enough to eat. As for my habiliments, look and see how I am accoutred," and he pointed to his faded and thread-bare doublet.

Le Grain, a contemporary, writes, "I have seen the king with a plain doublet of white stuff, all soiled by his cuirass and torn at the sleeve, and with well-worn breeches, unsewn on the side of the sword-belt."

While the king was thus destitute, the members of the council of finance were practicing gross extortion, and living in extravagance. The king was naturally light-hearted and gay, but the deplorable condition of the kingdom occasionally plunged him into the deepest of melancholy. A lady of the court one day remarked to him that he looked sad.

"Indeed," he replied, "how can I be otherwise, to see a people so ungrateful toward their king? Though I have done and still do all I can for them, and though for their welfare I would willingly sacrifice a thousand lives had God given me so many, as I have often proved, yet they daily attempt my life."

The council insisted that it was not safe for the king to leave so many of the Leaguers in the city, and urged their banishment. The king refused, saying,

"They are all my subjects, and I wish to love them equally."

The king now resolved, notwithstanding strong opposition from the Catholics, to place his illustrious Protestant friend, Sully, at the head of the ministry of finance. Sully entered upon his Herculean task with shrewdness which no cunning could baffle, and with integrity which no threat or bribe could bias. All the energies of calumny, malice, and violence were exhausted upon him, but this majestic man moved straight on, heedless of the storm, till he caused order to emerge from apparently inextricable confusion, and, by just and healthy measures, replenished the bankrupt treasury of the state.

The king was now pushing the siege of Amiens, which had for some time been in the hands of his enemies. During this time he wrote to his devoted friend and faithful minister of finance,

"I am very near the enemy, yet I have scarcely a horse upon which I can fight, or a suit of armor to put on. My doublet is in holes at the elbows. My kettle is often empty. For these two last days I have dined with one and another as I could. My purveyors inform me that they have no longer the means of supplying my table."

On the twenty-fifth of June, 1597, Amiens capitulated.

One of the kings of England is said to have remarked to his son, who was eager to ascend the throne, "Thou little knowest, my child, what a heap of cares and sorrows thou graspest at." History does, indeed, prove that "uneasy lies the head that wears a crown." New perplexities now burst upon the king. The Protestants, many of them irritated by his conversion, and by the tardy and insufficient concessions they received, violently demanded entire equality with the Catholics. This demand led to the famous Edict of Nantes. This ordinance, which receives its name from the place where it was published, was issued in the month of April, 1598. It granted to the Protestants full private liberty of conscience. It also permitted them to enjoy public worship in all places where the right was already established. Protestant lords of the highest rank could celebrate divine service in their castles with any number of their retainers. Nobles of the second rank might maintain private worship in their mansions, to which thirty persons could be admitted. Protestants were pronounced to be eligible to public office. Their children were to be admitted to the schools, their sick to the hospitals, and their poor to a share of the public charities. In a few specified places they were permitted to print books. Such, in the main, was the celebrated "Edict of Nantes."

The Catholics considered this an enormous and atrocious concession to deadly heresy. New clamors blazed forth against Henry, as in heart false to the Church. The Catholic clergy, in one combined voice, protested against it, and Pope Clement VIII. declared the Edict of Nantes, which permitted *liberty of conscience to every one, the most execrable that was ever made*.

It has required centuries of blood and woe to teach even a few individuals the true principles of religious liberty. Even in Protestant lands, the masses of the people have not yet fully learned that lesson. All over Catholic Europe, and all through the realms of paganism, intolerance still sways her cruel and bloody sceptre. These miserable religious wars in France, the birth of ignorance, fanaticism, and depravity, for seventy years polluted the state with gory scaffolds and blazing stakes. Three thousand millions of dollars were expended in the senseless strife, and two millions of lives were thrown away. At the close of the war, one half of the towns and the majestic castles of beautiful France were but heaps of smouldering ruins. All industry was paralyzed. The fields were abandoned to weeds and barrenness. The heart and the mind of the whole nation was thoroughly demoralized. Poverty, emaciation, and a semi-barbarism deformed the whole kingdom.

Neither the Catholics nor Protestants were satisfied with the Edict of Nantes. The Parliament of Paris, composed almost entirely of Catholics, for a long time refused its ratification. Henry called the courts before him, and insisted with kindness, but with firmness, that the edict should be verified.

"Gentlemen," said he, in the long speech which he made upon the occasion, "there must be no more distinction between Catholics and Protestants. All must be good Frenchmen. Let the Catholics convert the Protestants by the example of a good life. I am a shepherd-king, who will not shed the blood of his sheep, but who will seek to bring them all with kindness into the same fold."

The Catholic Parliament, thus constrained, finally adopted the edict. The Protestants also, perceiving clearly that this was the best that the king could do for them, after long discussion in their Consistory, which was, in reality, their Parliament, finally gave in their adhesion. The adjoining hostile powers, having no longer a party in France to join them, were thus disarmed. They sent embassadors to promote peace. Friendly treaties were speedily formed, and Henry was the undisputed monarch of a kingdom in repose.

Henry now commenced, with great energy, the promotion of the prosperity of his exhausted kingdom. To check the warlike spirit which had so long been dominant, he forbade any of his subjects, except his guards, to carry arms. The army was immediately greatly reduced, and public expenditures so diminished as materially to lighten the weight of taxation. Many of the nobles claimed exemption from the tax, but Henry was inflexible that the public burden should be borne equally by all. The people, enjoying the long unknown blessings of peace, became enthusiastically grateful to their illustrious benefactor.

In the month of October, 1598, the king was taken dangerously ill. The whole nation was in a panic. The touching demonstrations which Henry then received of the universal love and homage of his subjects affected him deeply. But few men find enough happiness in this world to lead them to cling very tenaciously to life when apparently on a dying bed. Henry at this time said to his attendants,

"I have no fear of death. I do not shrink at all from the great journey to the spirit land. But I greatly regret being removed from my beloved country before I have restored it to complete prosperity."

Happily, the fever was subdued, and he again, with indefatigable diligence, resumed his labors. To discourage the extravagance of the nobles, he set the example of extreme economy in all his personal expenses. He indulged in no gaudy equipage, his table was very frugally served, and his dress was simple in the extreme. No man in the kingdom devoted more hours to labor. He met his council daily, and in all their conferences exhibited a degree of information, shrewdness, and of comprehensive statesmanship which astonished the most experienced politicians who surrounded him.

It was a fierce battle which the king and his minister were compelled to fight for many years against the haughty nobles, who had ever regarded the mass of the people but as beasts of burden, made to contribute to their pleasure. The demands of these proud aristocrats were incessant and inexorable. It is a singular fact that, among them all, there was not a more thorough-going aristocrat than Sully himself. He had a perfect contempt for the people as to any power of self-government. They were, in his view, but sheep, to be carefully protected by a kind shepherd. It was as absurd, he thought, to consult them, as it would be for a shepherd to ask the advice of his flock. But Sully wished to take good care of the people, to shield them from all unequal burdens, from all aristocratic usurpations, and to protect them with inflexible justice in person and in property. His government was absolute in the extreme.

The Marchioness of Verneuil, in a towering rage, bitterly reproached the duke for preventing her from receiving a monopoly from the king, which would have secured to her an income of some five hundred thousand dollars a year.

"Truly the king will be a great fool," exclaimed the enraged marchioness, "if he continues to follow your advice, and thus alienates so many distinguished families. On whom, pray, should the king confer favors, if not on his relatives and his influential friends?"

"What you say," replied the unbending minister, "would be reasonable enough if his majesty took the money all out of his own purse. But to assess a new tax upon the merchants, artisans, laborers, and country people will never do. It is by them that the king and all of us are supported, and it is enough that they provide for a master, without having to maintain his cousins and friends."

For twelve years Henry, with his illustrious minister, labored with unintermitted zeal for the good of France. His love of France was an ever-glowing and growing passion for which every thing was to be surrendered. Henry was great in all respects but one. He was a slave to the passion of love. "And no one," says Napoleon, "can surrender himself to the passion of love without forfeiting some palms of glory." This great frailty has left a stain upon his reputation which truth must not conceal, which the genius of history with sorrow regards, and which can never be effaced. He was a great statesman. His heart was warm and generous. His philanthropy was noble and all-embracing, and his devotion to the best welfare of France was sincere and intense. Witness the following memorable prayer as he was just entering upon a great battle:

"O Lord, if thou meanest this day to punish me for my sins, I bow my head to the stroke of thy justice. Spare not the guilty. But, Lord, by thy holy mercy, have pity on this poor realm, and strike not the flock for the fault of the shepherd."

"If God," said he at another time, "shall grant me the ordinary term of human life, I hope to see France in such a condition that every peasant shall be able to have a fowl in the pot on Sunday."

This memorable saying shows both the benevolence of the king and the exceeding poverty, at that time, of the peasantry of France. Sully, in speaking of the corruption which had prevailed and of the measures of reform introduced, says,

"The revenue annually paid into the royal treasury was thirty millions. It could not be, I thought, that such a sum could reduce the kingdom of France so low. I resolved to enter upon the immense investigation. To my horror, I found that for these thirty millions given to his majesty there were extorted from the purses of his subjects, I almost blush to say, one hundred and fifty millions. After this I was no longer ignorant whence the misery of the people proceeded. I applied my cares to the authors of this oppression, who were the governors and other officers of the army, who all, even to the meanest, abused, in an enormous manner, their authority over the people. I immediately caused a decree to be issued, by which they were prohibited, under great penalties, to exact any thing from the people, under any title whatever, without a warrant in form."

The king co-operated cordially with his minister in these rigorous acts of reform, and shielded him with all the power of the monarchy from the storm of obloquy which these measures drew down upon him. The proud Duke of Epernon, exasperated beyond control, grossly insulted Sully. Henry immediately wrote to his minister, "If Epernon challenges you, I will be your second."

KARTINDO PUBLISHING HOUSE (Kartindo.Com)

The amiable, but sinning and consequently wretched Gabrielle was now importunate for the divorce, that she might be lawfully married to the king. But the children already born could not be legitimated, and Sully so clearly unfolded to the king the confusion which would thus be introduced, and the certainty that, in consequence of it, a disputed succession would deluge France in blood, that the king, ardently as he loved Gabrielle, was compelled to abandon the plan. Gabrielle was inconsolable, and inveighed bitterly against Sully. The king for a moment forgot himself, and cruelly retorted,

"Know, woman, that a minister like Sully must be dearer to me than even such a friend as you."

This harshness broke the heart of the unhappy Gabrielle. She immediately left Fontainebleau, where she was at that time with the king, and retired to Paris, saying, as she bade Henry adieu, "We shall never meet again." Her words proved true. On reaching Paris she was seized with convulsions, gave birth to a lifeless child, and died. Poor Gabrielle! Let compassion drop a tear over her grave! She was by nature one of the most lovely and noble of women. She lived in a day of darkness and of almost universal corruption. Yielding to the temptation of a heroic monarch's love, she fell, and a subsequent life of sorrow was terminated by an awful death, probably caused by poison.

Henry, as soon as informed of her sickness, mounted his horse to gallop to Paris. He had proceeded but half way when he was met by a courier who informed him that Gabrielle was dead. The dreadful blow staggered the king, and he would have fallen from his horse had he not been supported by his attendants. He retired to Fontainebleau, shut himself up from all society, and surrendered himself to the most bitter grief. Sully in vain endeavored to console him. It was long before he could turn his mind to any business. But there is no pain whose anguish time will not diminish. New cares and new loves at length engrossed the heart where Gabrielle had for a few brief years so supremely reigned.

The utterly profligate Marguerite, now that Gabrielle was dead, whom she of course hated, was perfectly willing to assent to a divorce. While arrangements were making to accomplish this end, the king chanced to meet a fascinating, yet pert and heartless coquette, Henriette d'Entragues, daughter of Francis Balzac, Lord of Entragues. Though exceedingly beautiful, she was a calculating, soulless girl, who was glad of a chance to sell herself for rank and money. She thus readily bartered her beauty to the king, exacting, with the most cool financiering, as the price, a written promise that he would marry her as soon as he should obtain a divorce from Marguerite of Valois, upon condition that she, within the year, should bear him a son.

The king, having written the promise, placed it in the hands of Sully. The bold minister read it, then tore it into fragments. The king, amazed at such boldness, exclaimed in a passion, "Sir, I believe that you are mad."

"True, sire, I am," replied Sully; "but would to God that I were the only madman in France."

But Henry, notwithstanding his anger, could not part from a minister whose services were so invaluable. He immediately drew up another promise, which he placed in the hands of the despicable beauty. This rash and guilty pledge was subsequently the cause of great trouble to the king.

Henry having obtained a divorce, the nation demanded that he should form a connection which should produce a suitable heir to inherit the throne. Thus urged, and as Henrietta did not give birth to the wished-for son, Henry reluctantly married, in the year 1600, Maria of Medici, niece of the Grand Duke of Tuscany.

Maria was a domineering, crafty, ambitious woman, who embittered the life of the king. She was very jealous, and with reason enough, of the continued influence of Henrietta; and the palace was the scene of disgraceful domestic broils. Henry, in one of his letters to Sully, describes the queen as "terribly robust and healthy." But when she gave birth to a son who was undeniably heir to the throne, thus allaying the fears of a disputed succession, the whole nation rejoiced, and Henry became somewhat reconciled to his unattractive spouse. The king was exceedingly fond of this child. One day the Spanish embassador, a dignified Castilian, was rather suddenly ushered into the royal presence at Fontainebleau. The monarch was on all fours on the floor, running about the room with the little dauphin on his back. Raising his eyes, he said to the embassador,

"Are you a father?"

"Yes, sire," was the reply.

"Then I may finish my play," said Henry, and he took another trot around the room.

Henrietta and her relatives were greatly exasperated that the king did not fulfill his promise of marriage. The father and daughter, joined by the Count d'Auvergne, plotted against the king's life. They were arrested and condemned to death. The king, however, transmuted their punishment to exile.

One of the grandest schemes of Henry deserves particular mention. Reflecting deeply upon the wars with which Europe had ever been desolated, and seeing the occasion for this in the innumerable states and nations into which Europe was divided, of various degrees of power, and each struggling for its own selfish interest, he proposed to unite all the states of Europe in one vast Christian Republic. The whole continent was to be divided into fifteen states, as uniform in size and power as possible. These states were to be, according to their choice, monarchical or republican. They were to be associated on a plan somewhat resembling that of the United States of America.

Nothing can more conclusively show the entire absence of correct notions of religious toleration prevailing at that day than the plan proposed to prevent religious quarrels. Wherever any one form of faith predominated, that was to be maintained as the national faith. In Catholic states, there were to be no Protestants; in Protestant states, no Catholics. The minority, however, were not to be exterminated; they were only to be compelled to emigrate to the countries where their own form of faith prevailed. All pagans and Mohammedans were to be driven out of Europe into Asia. To enforce this change, an army of two hundred and seventy thousand infantry, fifty thousand cavalry, two hundred cannon, and one hundred and twenty ships of war, was deemed amply sufficient.

The first step was to secure the co-operation of two or three of the most powerful kings of Europe. This would render success almost certain. Sully examined the plan with the utmost care in all its details. Henry wished first to secure the approval of England, Sweden, and Denmark.

But, in the midst of these schemes of grandeur, Henry was struck down by the hand of an assassin. On the fourteenth of May, 1610, the king left the Louvre at four o'clock in the afternoon to visit Sully, who was sick. Preparations were making for the public entry of the queen, who, after a long delay, had just been crowned. The city was thronged; the day was fine, and the curtains of the coach were drawn up. Several nobles were in the spacious carriage with the king. As

KARTINDO PUBLISHING HOUSE (Kartindo.Com)

the coach was turning out of the street Honoré into the narrow street Ferronnerie, it was stopped by two carts which blocked up the way. Just at that instant a man from the crowd sprang upon a spoke of the wheel, and struck a dagger into the king just above the heart. Instantly repeating the blow, the heart was pierced. Blood gushed from the wound and from the mouth of the king, and, without uttering a word, he sank dead in the arms of his friends.

The wretched assassin, a fanatic monk, was immediately seized by the guard. With difficulty they protected him from being torn to pieces by the infuriated people. His name was Francis Ravaillac. According to the savage custom of the times, he was subsequently put to death with the most frightful tortures.

The lifeless body of the king was immediately taken to the Tuileries and placed upon a bed. Surgeons and physicians hurried to the room only to gaze upon his corpse. No language can depict the grief and despair of France at his death. He had won the love of the whole nation, and, to the present day, no one hears the name of Henry the Fourth mentioned in France but with affection. He was truly the father of his people. All conditions, employments, and professions were embraced in his comprehensive regard. He spared no toil to make France a happy land. He was a man of genius and of instinctive magnanimity. In conversation he had no rival. His profound and witty sayings which have been transmitted to us are sufficient to form a volume. His one great and almost only fault sadly tarnishes his otherwise fair and honorable fame.

In Henry commenced the reign of the house of Bourbon. For nearly two hundred years the family retained the crown. It is now expelled, and the members are wandering in exile through foreign lands.

There is one great truth which this narrative enforces: it is the doctrine of *freedom of conscience*. It was the denial of this simple truth which deluged France in blood and woe. The recognition of this one sentiment would have saved for France hundreds of thousands of lives, and millions of treasure. Let us take warning. We need it.

Let us emblazon upon our banner the noble words, "*Toleration--perfect civil and religious toleration.*" But Toleration is not a slave. It is a spirit of light and of liberty. It has much to give, but it has just as much to demand. It bears the olive-branch in one hand, and the gleaming sword in the other. I grant *to you*, it says, perfect liberty of opinion and of expression, and I demand *of you* the same.

Let us then inscribe upon the arch which spans our glorious Union, making us one in its celestial embrace, *"Freedom of speech, freedom of the press, and free men."*

Then shall that arch beam upon us like God's bow of promise in the cloud, proclaiming that this land shall never be deluged by the surges of civil war-- that it never shall be inundated by flames and blood.

The human mind is now so roused that it will have this liberty; and if there are any institutions of religion or of civil law which can not stand this scrutiny, they are doomed to die. The human mind will move with untrammeled sweep through the whole range of religious doctrine, and around the whole circumference and into the very centre of all political assumptions.

If the Catholic bishop have a word to say, let him say it. If some one, rising in the spirit and power of Martin Luther, has a reply to make, let him make it. Those who wish to listen to the one or the other, let them do so. Those who wish to close their ears, let them have their way.

Our country is one. Our liberty is national. Let us then grant toleration every where throughout our wide domain, in Maine and in Georgia, amid the forests of the Aroostook and upon the plains of Kansas.

THE END

KARTINDO PUBLISHING HOUSE (Kartindo.Com)

www.ingramcontent.com/pod-product-compliance
Lightning Source LLC
Chambersburg PA
CBHW060518290526
45791CB00001B/437